EVANG.
THE COUNTER-REVOLUTION

EVANGELISM—

THE
COUNTER-REVOLUTION

Lewis A. Drummond

MARSHALL, MORGAN & SCOTT
London

MARSHALL, MORGAN & SCOTT
BLUNDELL HOUSE
GOODWOOD ROAD
LONDON SE14 6BL

ISBN 0 551 05177 9

Printed in Great Britain by The Anchor Press Ltd,
and bound by Wm. Brendon & Son Ltd,
both of Tiptree, Essex

This book is affectionately dedicated to

MY WIFE

who has been the kind of pastor's wife this pastor has
needed to carry out his ministry and service for our
Lord Jesus Christ.

Foreword

To have Dr Drummond asking me to write a foreword to a book of his on the subject of the pastor-evangelist is rather like being asked by Jack Nicklaus to write a foreword to a book he had written on golf. A casual flick through the pages of this book will show that Dr Drummond has command of his subject and can present his case in a very readable manner.

Dr Drummond is one of the few American pastors in recent years who has come to Britain and really lived and worked amongst us. When he suggests innovations and courses of action for our Church strategy he speaks with a knowledge of what our situation is really like.

The book will give the reader ample evidence of Dr Drummond's happy blend of scholarship and practical experience and above all his great enthusiasm for the cause of the gospel. Like him I believe that the local church must be a focal point for continuous evangelism. The problem is how such an ideal can be realised. To put up signs, open our doors and provide effective speakers is not the real answer; firstly because the people we most want to reach are hardly likely to come, and secondly—as Dr Drummond believes passionately—because it obscures a better way. Every committed church member is meant to play a part in God's mission to our world. Although I believe that some of us are especially gifted as evangelists, there is a sense in which all of us can play a part in evangelism. For this to happen there needs to be—the pastor-evangelist. I think that we in Britain have been a little slow to see this, and as one who has held a pastorate I am as guilty as anyone if this is so.

Tied in with the ideal of the pastor-evangelist is the whole concept of Christian education. There is a tremendous need for the British Church to take the teaching and training of its members more seriously. The average Christian freely admits to a great deal of ignorance concerning basic aspects of his belief. Again, my guess is that relatively few clergy are following a systematic programme of Christian education in their churches. I fear that we are reaping exactly what we have sown. Dr Drummond belongs to the Southern Baptist Convention of the U.S.A. who are renowned for their thoroughness in these matters and therefore we can expect him to have something worth saying—and he has.

I am particularly happy to write these words of introduction because it highlights something which I believe is important for today's Church to learn. Dr Drummond is a Baptist and I am an Anglican. Whenever I have met and talked with him we have experienced Christian unity. I am convinced that unity cannot be separated from the biblical gospel and biblical evangelism. If this book could stimulate the cause of evangelism in our churches then I am convinced Christians will find themselves closer to each other than by the pursuit of any other course.

GAVIN REID

Contents

Preface

There is perhaps no theme that has captured the interest of the contemporary Church quite as profoundly as the concept of evangelism. That which was once pushed aside or ignored by many has now become the interest of most enlightened Christians. There are probably many reasons for this renewed concern in mission. And although it may well be true that some of the motives that have spurred this concern are not as high or spiritual as one would wish, none the less, the theme of evangelism is of vital interest to most Christians today and for that we must be grateful.

The purpose of this volume on the subject of mission is quite simple. It is to place in the hands of the pastor and Christian leader a basic work on the essential aspects of the evangelistic enterprise and to provide foundational guidelines on how to evangelise in a local church. Thus it has a practical as well as a theological purpose. The primary theme of the book is that the pastor stands at the very fountain head of the evangelistic tide in a church. He holds the key to successful mission. He, therefore, must become a 'pastor-evangelist' in a deep and profound sense. Elucidating this essential truth, the book then attempts to guide the pastor and his church into a dynamic evangelistic programme.

I must not close this brief preface without expressing my gratitude to those whose help has been invaluable.

Dr James D. Williams, of the Southwestern Baptist Theological Seminary in Fort Worth, Texas, read the manuscript and made extremely helpful suggestions. My typists, Mrs James D. Williams and Miss Irene Butler, were obviously of great assistance. To these I acknowledge my debt. So I simply present my concept of the evangelistic task with the prayer that God will use it to inspire and help us all to 'do the work of an evangelist' (2 Tim. 4:5).

L.A.D.

Spurgeon's College
London
1972

I

The Role of the Pastor in Evangelism

Rip Van Winkle, the fictitious short story penned by Washington Irving during the American romantic movement in literature, has a startling relevance for the Church today. The intriguing little tale tells of Rip Van Winkle, something of an early American village character, who went hunting one afternoon into the Kaatskill Mountains. Being fatigued by his hike up the hills, he stretched out on a grassy knoll to rest. He was soon asleep. When he finally awoke he discovered to his amazement that he had slept through what he thought was the night. He hurried back into town, but there strange sights began to greet his eyes. Old familiar landmarks were either gone or radically changed. He seemed to recognise no one. After a brush with the local citizenry at a political rally that was taking place in the town square when Rip entered the village, it began to dawn on him that he had not slept through the night as he supposed. Rather, he had been slumbering for twenty years, during which time the thirteen British colonies of the Empire had become the thirteen newly formed United States of America. Poor old Rip had slept through a revolution.

The fact that the Church today is living and attempting to minister in a revolutionary atmosphere is patent to all. Everything appears to be radically changing. All aspects of society are in flux. Every foundation is being shaken. No segment of the so-called Establishment escapes being questioned. The only certainty seems to be that nothing will ever be the same again. But the most disquieting element of this sociological revolution is that often the 'sleeping Rip Van Winkle' of the hour is none other than the Church. Christians, who should be on the very cutting edge of this changing scene and moving society towards God, are often found slumbering away on some grassy knoll of irrelevance or unrealistic traditionalism while the world all but explodes and fragments around them.

In the light of such a situation it is therefore vital for the Church to come alive to the contemporary sociological scene and address itself to the problems this social revolution precipitates. Now, I do not think it can be correctly said that the Church is completely dead and thus ready for a decent burial as some critics advocate. Rather, it more or less finds itself, at least in some of its institutionalised forms, in the grip of irrelevancy and needs to be awakened and updated. And if God's people can be shaken from their slumbers and made to see and respond to the evangelistic challenge of this turbulent hour, great things can yet be done. Moreover, it may just be that the disturbing voices being heard today will be those which will disturb this sleep.

The voices being heard in contemporary society
A voice that is being currently heard loud and clear by the masses is that of a secular scientism with a purely empirical, rational approach to all of life. Those who advocate this line see truth and reality in only those things which the five senses and rationalism can verify. Strangely, even many contemporary philosophers have enrolled in this school. The result is that the great and vitally important metaphysical questions that philosophy has always grappled with are now banned from philosophical discussion. These thinkers take this rigid, empirical line because such metaphysical discussion

14

raises questions, the answers to which are not verifiable rationally or empirically. And virtually every university philosophical department in Europe and America is more or less relatively committed to some form of linguistic, empirical thought. The result is that philosophy has suffered correspondingly as it has ignored many vital issues. Of course, the average man in the street obviously shares in this attitude. He is often all too clearly a pragmatic empiricist, even if implicitly. Thus it seems that today both the sophisticated and the common man alike all but worship at the shrine of a scientific approach to truth and reality.

Certainly no one wishes to decry the amazing advance and tremendous benefit that scientific empirical investigation has produced. We all enjoy, and rightly so, these good things of the affluent society. But many have built their entire system of values on this level, and this is where the problems begin. Ignoring the reality of spiritual values, they define security on a purely materialistic basis. Health and wholeness are sought in scientific medicine and behaviouristic psychology *alone*. Status, and therefore acceptance by one's peers, means the attainment of economic levels. In the spirit of Hegel, who claimed everything for his pure rationalism, these devotees of empirical science believe that all problems, in principle if not yet in fact, can finally be solved in the laboratory or on the psychiatrist's couch. And though the common man may not be able, as the philosopher can, to present a formal rationale for his completely empirical, rational approach to reality, he certainly lives out on a practical level those basic presuppositions.

The pressing problem for evangelism that this situation precipitates is that the Church must find a convincing apologetic for our faith in this empirical and rationalistic scientific atmosphere. For example, the so-called conflict between science and religion that has caused many young people to cast their vote for the laboratory instead of the pulpit must be resolved. And it cannot be done by arguing on the level that many Christians do today, namely, never getting down to the essential presuppositions of what truth is. Schaeffer has correctly pointed out :

> The floodwaters of secular thought ... overwhelmed the Church because the leaders did not understand the importance of combating a false set of presuppositions. They largely fought the battle on the wrong ground and so, instead of being far ahead in both defence and communication, they lagged woefully behind. . . . Man thinks differently concerning truth, and *so now for us, more than ever before, a presuppositional apologetic is imperative.*[1]

The place of apologetics in evangelism is, of course, a subject in itself. What is essential to see at this point is that unless we can help the present, and especially the next generation—which is, as never before, a 'thinking' generation—to find a resolution to the supposed antithesis between empirical rationalism and the Christian faith, we shall lose many for Christ and His Church.

Another voice being heard today is somewhat in contrast to the appeal of empirical science. This voice can probably be called, because a label is convenient, atheistic existentialism. The existentialist, in over-simplified terms, sees existence as more important than essence. So one is urged to find reality and meaning in one's human experience. Drain from each moment of existence all the good it has to offer, they tell us. Now this line of thought, rather than leading to a kind of proud utopianism and optimism as scientific empiricism tends to do, leads many to a serious and almost morbid despair. They discover that much of the chaos of this world seems to give no reality, order or meaning. Thus, because they fail to look beyond the immediacy of their temporal existence, deep despair can easily ensue. But still, the practical result of this orientation to life is in essence the same as for the hard-nosed empiricist, namely, no God. As Heidegger has expressed it, we came from nothing and we go to nothing. Thus one is constantly thrown back on his own self. Of course, it may be true that not all who live in this general frame of reference are propositional atheists. Yet they are surely practical atheists as far as pragmatic living is concerned.

At the same time, these advocates have rejected philosophical rationalism, and in a modified sense, even empiricism, as a way to truth and meaning. But the crunch for the Church is, they also reject the concept of revealed truth which is clearly the Christian position. Thus with little or nothing left to build upon except their own selves, they just opt out. This is their decision of 'courage' in order to become an 'authentic self'.

As is evident, here is where we find the modern hippie movement. Granted that many of them have not thought out their position in philosophical terms, yet this is still their basic approach to life. And if the Church thinks this group is just long-haired, dirty and reactionary and should thus be held up to scorn and contempt, it is going to miss envangelising a rapidly growing segment of society. A cursory survey of almost every facet of contemporary life should tell us this. Existential philosophy is almost dominating the field of modern music, the arts, the theatre, etc. Few young people are free from its influence. They all read Camus, Sartre, and others. They all love the pop music of the Beatles and other groups. They all 'dig' modern art. Thus we who would evangelise must come to grips with this tremendously influential issue. And how we should thank God for the evidence of awakening as reflected in the 'Jesus People'. This movement could well be one of the greatest challenges the Church has faced for many years. I trust God's people will rise to the hour and meet the needs of this challenge and make their contribution to it.

A third voice that presently sallies forth is humanism, i.e. the concept which holds that life is to be understood in purely human terms alone. There have always been humanists, of course. But they have usually tended to stay in their ivory towers or in relatively small esoteric groups. Perhaps the reason humanism as an orientation to life has come down to the market place in this generation is in some sense because of the influence of behaviouristic psychology. It may be true that the influence of behaviourism was essentially negative in that it eliminated for many the relevance, if not the concept, of God. But this movement, coupled with the industrial revolution and its depersonalisation of man, caused the human character to cry out desperately for recognition. Thus today we have a sort of romantic materialistic view of human personality. Growing out of this basic approach to existence, humanism consequently says that all that is real and of ultimate value are the human personality and human interests. And this has clearly been a growing life view, especially since Freud. Naturally, as is the case with science and existentialism, there is a genuine element of truth in humanism. All Christians should find sympathy with philanthropical endeavours to enhance human dignity and meet the pressing needs of our fellow-men. Persons are important, vitally important. But when materialistic humanism becomes a world view that excludes God and spiritual values as the ultimate good and romanticises about man and his accomplishments, that is when trouble begins for the evangel. And this is one of the current life views we find and with which the Church must cope.

Perhaps the most disturbing issue to the average Christian is the strange milieu in which contemporary ethics finds itself. This is largely due, I believe, to the present-day spirit of 'relativism', i.e. the idea that there are no such things as absolutes. This basic presupposition has all but taken the hour. Even the traditional systems of logic and truth have fallen. As we know, the first move in classical logical thought is: if you have 'A' it is not 'Non-A'. But as Schaeffer says, 'if you understand the extent to which this no longer holds sway, you will understand our present situation.'[2] Everything is relative; there are no absolutes, we are told. Therefore, there are no *absolute* ethical or moral principles. It is in something of this atmosphere that the so-called situation ethic emerged with its rejection of objective, absolute standards. As young people are urged to 'do their thing', established principles of moral right and wrong are rejected. As Harvey Cox has advocated in more philosophical terms, 'There is no reason that man must believe the ethical standards he lives by came down from heaven inscribed on golden tablets. He can accept the fact that value systems, like states and civilisations, come and go. They are conditioned by their history and claim no finality.'[3]

It is obviously true that certain Victorian concepts needed to fall. But because of the spirit of relativism in ethics, many of the great biblical principles of moral right have been swept away in the avalanche. In the light of this disappearance of objective, securely grounded values, it is little wonder that Tillich called this world a 'land of broken symbols'. The consequence of it all is that today there is such confusion in ethics that everyone seems to be in a state of moral turmoil from the thinker in his isolated study to the hippie in his communal group. If ever an age were ethically and morally adrift on a sea of uncertainty, this is that age.

Another strange aspect of the moral confusion of the moment is found in the fact that, generally speaking, those over forty see morals and ethics on more of an individual basis while the younger 'beat generation' sees them on a larger social level. Thus older adults tend to hold in contempt young people who demonstrate for a very worthy moral or social issue, because after the demonstration they may go to bed together. And by the same token young people display contempt for the older view of sexual morality because many of its advocates are seemingly blind to the pressing moral social issues that have them 'turned on'. Consequently, both groups become rather lop-sided in their ethical concepts, for they fail to see that morals are individual *and* social. Thus the so-called generation gap widens. And, tragically, the Church seems less able to evangelise as this gap becomes wider.

Our day of ferment can probably best be summarised and described with that much used and confused word 'secularism'. It is simply that many people are living today as if God actually were dead, even though they may deny the radical ideas of Hamilton, Altizer, Van Buren and their kindred. And I would suppose that the average secularised man has a bit of all these current philosophies in his life view. There are few purists today. If Socrates was right when he said, 'The unexamined life is not worth living', Mr Average Man is living a pretty worthless life. Few have thought out in a systematic way their life-style—they just live it. Moreover, most people are just pragmatists. If a thing or thought works, they utilise it. The results are that the bulk of people live a simple, practical, secular life.

Rather strangely, this secular society philosophy has been met with widely divergent reactions within the thinking Christian community. There are those who see any sort of human emancipation as a threat to their dogmatically closed and extremely narrow world view. Surely this reaction is not the biblical answer, and therefore, no answer at all. But, conversely, there are those who herald this day as the day of redemption from old erroneous forms whose demise is long overdue. Society has at last 'come of age', they tell us. Thus a secularisation theology has emerged which advocates the rejection of *any* closed world view, especially a closed *theological* world view. As Harvey Cox has said, defining secularisation theology, 'It is the loosing of the world from religious and quasi-religious understandings of itself, the dispelling of all closed world-views, the breaking of all supernatural myths and sacred symbols. . . . It has

20

relativised religious world views and thus rendered them innocuous.'[4]

Yet, this position leaves one a bit uneasy in that several questions come to mind :

1. Is the presupposition (for it is a presupposition) that a closed world view is untenable a valid position? This is highly debatable.

2. Does not the Bible present what Cox calls a 'closed world view'? His arguments to the contrary are hardly convincing. (Cox's biblical exegesis seems woefully inadequate.)

3. Is not the whole secularisation philosophy something of a closed world view in itself? If we say everything is constantly in a state of flux, is not this a world view too? And if it is dogmatically held, does not that tend to close it?

4. Can one ever have any sort of tenable cosmology without it being something of a closed world view?

Be that as it may, it seems clear that a purely secularisation theology, despite its admirable aspects, is not the biblical view in the truest sense and thus will surely not give any lasting, satisfying answers to today's utter secularism. We shall be discussing this type of 'new theology' in more detail later. Suffice it to say here that I hold that secularisation theology will not bring secular man back to God in the biblical sense of what it means to be redeemed. The reason I take this position is because I feel that these theologians fail to supply adequate answers to the basic questions men are asking this hour, namely, 'Who am I?' and 'Where am I going?'

Now it is in this atmosphere that the Church is called upon to minister today. And the two basic questions cited above are what we are being asked by contemporary man. Thus the task of the Church is to present Christ to the world as we find it, not as it was or as we would like it, and communicate in a relevant manner that in Christ is to be found the answer to life's ultimate questions.

21

The growing ineffectiveness of the Church

Here is where the trouble begins, for it is clear that many churches have to some extent failed in their evangelistic responsibility. Moreover, it seems that this relative ineffectiveness to communicate the gospel to a rapidly changing world is a growing problem. This can be seen to a greater or lesser degree in the boycott of the institutionalised church by large masses of society. It is true that there is a general boycott of practically all institutions and an overall rebellion against everything that smacks of the Establishment. However, other institutions have not suffered quite like the churches. As pointed out by Paul Musselman, '. . . the dying urban churches are indications of an unplanned, but nevertheless real, protest by the urban disinherited. The streams of people who pass but never enter an urban church represents a form of unconscious picketing against the Church.'[5] But this disillusionment with institutionalism is not the only reason that people by-pass the churches today. And it surely cannot be used as an 'out' to excuse our lack of effective evangelism. There are many other reasons, two of which cannot be disregarded, for about these we can do something constructive. Therefore these issues must be courageously met.

Two issues to face

First, there is the Church's reluctance to change and thus to speak relevantly to our day. Let me illustrate this problematic attitude in this way : Not so long ago I was conducting a session on the theme of effective local church evangelism. The participants came from different churches and consisted largely of laymen. I was advocating changes in programmes and procedures that would aid in more effectively reaching people with the gospel. During the discussion period that followed, a layman suddenly burst out, 'What's wrong with meeting at eleven o'clock on Sunday morning for worship?'

I did not recall the hour of worship even being mentioned. Yet, here was a man so bound to a specific programme as he had known it that he was almost angered at the thought of any change, even one as minor as that and even if it meant ministering more effectively. But this attitude is not restricted to the layman alone. I was speaking to a group of ministers recently. In the course of the discussion that followed my address on pastoral evangelism and the need to update evangelistic methodology, I mentioned how all that the Victorian era implied is almost despised by many today. One minister rose to say that he did not concur with that line of thought at all. He felt most people still loved Victoriana as was indicated by their willingness to buy Victorian antiques. Of course, he did not realise the reason that Victorian antiques are popular is because of the fact that they are plentiful and cheap. The tragedy was, however, that here was a minister whose whole spirit implied that old methodologies must be kept regardless of their inadequacies. It was quite disturbing to sense how far he was removed from the realities and necessities of the day. If anyone should be alive to the contemporary scene and be ready for change, it should be ministers.

Of course, when one speaks of the necessity for overturning traditions, the reference is essentially to outmoded methodologies. The great traditions and theologies of Christianity *must* remain. The gospel itself is always unchanging. But every generation has the right to hear the good news communicated in a fashion that genuinely addresses its message in current forms and to man in his present sociological environment. For us today, this implies change—often drastic change—in our methods and programmes. Georgia Harkness has rightly said that '. . . if the Church is to win the battle against secularism by the sword of the Spirit, some deep-seated changes are in order.'[6] We can no longer conduct business as usual. True, the business is the same, but conducting it as usual is spelling death to many congregations, not to say what happens to the multitudes without Christ. It is as simple as that. I know that this issue has been discussed *ad infinitum*. But the time for discussion is surely over. Courageous action is demanded! If we are in any way to meet the demands of this revolutionary age, something of a counter-revolution must take place within the churches. And we can change significantly, if we will. Moreover, I would hope that some practical suggestions and guidelines will be found in these pages that will enable us to get started. But more of that later.

Secondly, there is another impediment to the Church's evangelistic ministry today. It centres in the somewhat 'uncertain sound' that some churches have trumpeted as to what the gospel truly is. Obviously, this is bewildering to people. The man in the street hears what is called the Church's message. But because of the diversity of 'gospels' he may hear, he does not know what to believe. Thus he loses confidence in the Church's claim to speak God's truth and proceeds to do 'what is right (or wrong) in his own eyes'. What is the gospel then? What is our message? In a word, it is that which is implied by the term *kerygma*. We shall discuss the theology of the *kerygma* in a subsequent chapter. May I simply summarise here and say the Church has only one clear note to sound to all, namely, 'Christ and him crucified' (1 Cor. 2 : 2). This is our good news. When this truth is heralded, men hear. It is true that we cannot dictate what others proclaim. But we can be sure that *our* message is that which men need most to understand. Our evangelism will never be successful or relevant until we declare Christ. This issue, too, we must face. In the light of this central truth, here is a good place to raise the question :

What is evangelism?
Recently, various writers have used the terms 'evangelism' or 'mission' rather fast and loose. To this point, I have used them frequently and quite freely. But a pre-

24

cise definition is important. In attempting to give a sound meaning to the word, an Anglican commission on evangelism said, 'To evangelise is so to present Christ Jesus in the power of the Holy Spirit that men shall come to put their trust in God through Him, to accept Him as their Saviour, and serve Him as their King in the fellowship of His Church.'[7] W. E. Sangster, the great Methodist preacher, tells us that 'Evangelism is going to the people outside. It is the proclamation of the good news of God in Jesus Christ to "Them that are without" . . . It is the sheer work of the herald who goes in the name of the King to the people who, either openly or by their indifference, deny their allegiance to their rightful Lord. He blows the trumpet and demands to be heard.'[8] Professor Schelling of Boston University states, 'Evangelism is the proclamation, in word or deed, of the "good news of Jesus Christ" with the aim of winning a positive response. It is the endeavour to bring persons wholeheartedly to accept and live by the redemptive love of God as revealed in Jesus Christ.'[9]

Douglas Webster points out in general terms that '. . . evangelism is the proclamation of the gospel'.[10] And we all know D. T. Niles' poignant definition that evangelism is simply 'one beggar telling another beggar where to find bread'. Perhaps the concept can be summarised and conveyed in this fashion : Evangelism is a concerted effort to confront the unbeliever with the truth about and claims of Jesus Christ so as to challenge and lead him into repentance toward God and faith in our Lord Jesus Christ and thus into the fellowship of the Church.

If we will grant that these definitions are valid from a biblical perspective, it is clear that the term 'evangelism' is used by many today in too broad a sense and by others in too narrow a manner. For example, evangelism is simply not everything we do, as some seem to understand it. Although the spirit of evangelism should permeate all Christian activity and ministry, everything we do is not evangelism *per se*. It can be rather self-deceptive to define evangelism too broadly. It can even be a subtle excuse for not engaging in outright, pointed evangelistic endeavours. Conversely, evangelism is surely far more than just formally 'preaching the gospel'. Communicating the good news is a much broader concept than doing no more than what the preacher does from the pulpit. It clearly implies action as well as proclamation. Moreover, the entire Church is to engage in it.

But there is our task; to evangelise a bewildered mass, caught up in a sociological revolution that has all but overturned every stabilising tradition. And we have surely found by now that 'we are heading for sure disaster in the Church of our contemporary society when we insist on forcing new wine into old wineskins'.[11] A new day is upon us and therefore a new challenge is before us. And what a challenge it is! Will we win the day for Christ? That is the most pressing question we face. There are those who say no. But I believe the Church still has a real measure of vitality in it, and I surely believe God can do mighty things—and do those things through His people. Yet to see the desperately needed renewal of the Church and a new and dynamic impetus for outreach, it seems vital that we must come to grips with

A theology of church-centred evangelism
It is axiomatic that the first principle to recognise in a theology of church-centred evangelism rests in the fact that *outreach* is the Church's primary mission in the world. Of course, this does not state the case quite properly. Actually, the mission is God's mission. The Church merely shares in the *missio Dei*. But in this secondary sense it does have such a mission and the Church has been commissioned to the task by our Lord Himself. Surely all would agree that Jesus's statement in Matthew 28 : 19–20 is foundational to the very life and ministry of the Church. And these words are clearly

26

the words of evangelism: 'Go forth therefore and make all nations my disciples; baptise men everywhere in the name of the Father and the Son and the Holy Spirit, and teach them to observe all that I have commanded you. And be assured, I am with you always, to the end of time' (N.E.B.). Thus the Church shares in the *missio Dei* and in so doing lives close to the heart of God. It would seem today that no apologetic is needed to convince the knowledgeable Christian and pastor that mission is the core of the local church's ministry. On the contrary, evangelism and its study has become one of the contemporary Church's keenest interests.

Simply put then, God is the Divine Missionary, i.e. God is on a mission of world redemption. And His basic plan for world evangelisation is the use of the instrumentality of the Church. This is why it is so clear in the Scriptures that, as Whitesell tells us, 'New Testament local churches were nerve centres of evangelism, and in this respect constitute a pattern for local churches of all ages. Missionary evangelism had produced these local churches, and they in turn made evangelism and missionary activity their main business.'[12]

Pastors and laymen with insight have long recognised this truth. Yet it appears that the Church *as a whole* has failed to grasp in depth the importance and reality of its call to mission. But surely it is God's expectation that the *entire* Church be involved in the task. As Leighton Ford has said, 'If our goal is the penetration of the whole world; then for the agents to carry out the task we must aim at nothing less than *the mobilisation of the whole Church*.'[13] What then will wake the whole Church from its dogmatic and traditional slumbers and motivate it to fulfil its ministry?

We shall discuss the problem of apathy in more detail later, but it can be said here that it would obviously help if the Church could come alive to the revolution society is undergoing. This is why several pages were given to a diagnosis of this scene. It seems rather strange, actually, that the Church, which is itself a real part of society and thus to some extent sharing in the revolution, has developed something of a ghetto mentality. But until the Church is aware of the contemporary scene and that it is to minister in a preserving capacity, it will find extreme difficulty in becoming the 'Church for others'. As the report of the Western European Working Group of the Department on Studies in Evangelism aptly pointed out:

> Faced with secular society, with the understanding of history as involving constant change and transformation and with the acknowledgement that the Church has to turn itself outwards to the world, we are summoned in the present age, as in any age, to test the traditions of the churches and their own self-understanding.

For, surely today:

> One may say we are in danger of perpetuating 'come-structures' instead of replacing them by 'go-structures'. One may say that inertia has replaced the dynamism of the Gospel and of participation in the mission of God. . . . Because of this inertia and this insulation from the world, we have come to exist beside and often outside the reality of the world, instead of being present in its structures. Our own structures then operate as obstacles and hindrances preventing the proclamation of the Gospel reaching mankind.[14]

Yet, regardless of the present problems within and without, we have learned that it is the Church that God basically uses to accomplish the task. This has invariably been the divine plan, and I suppose always will be. With its often archaic structures, its apathy, its reluctance to change and its thousand and one other diffi-

28

culties, the Church still remains as the one to 'stand in the gap' and minister Christ to the world.* Moreover, as I have already implied before, I do not share with some the utter despair they feel for the contemporary Church. I believe the Western European Working Group was correct when it emphasised that part of the mission of the Church is to renew itself. Further, the Holy Spirit is constantly moving the Church towards renewal and resurrection. And there are many signs that point in the direction of renewal being upon us, for instance a vast new interest in evangelism, ministers gathering in clinics on outreach, departments of evangelism cropping out in various church structures. All of these things should encourage those committed to evangelism. Perhaps we are on the edge of a new world-wide gospel thrust. It could just be that the counter-revolution we are calling for is beginning. To that end one would surely hope and pray.

A new challenge needed
Still, there are painful days ahead. The Church is not going to be revolutionised so as to cope with the revolution outside until some forthright and courageous challenges are presented to it. And from what quarter will such a call and challenge come? It seems self-evident from what quarter it *should* come, namely, the pastor. Therefore, it is most important for the informed layman

* However, when we make such a claim for the Church, let it be understood that this does not imply that God is at work *only* in and through the structures of the Church's current institutional forms. God is obviously working in the world in a thousand different ways. We can surely see what God is doing by reading reports from various organisations that labour for the betterment of the human lot as well as by reading the annual reports of our various denominational agencies. We can even read the daily newspapers and see the hand of God as He ministers to human need through others than the Church. This is one area of truth where the secularisation theologians are challenging us. And we should give pause to thank God for all He is doing and for our becoming increasingly aware of it. Yet, in the prime task of world evangelisation, it is still the Church that is the basic instrument of God.

29

as well as for the minister of the congregation to see that in a theology of church-centred evangelism every pastor has the key role.

The responsibility of the pastor as evangelist
This theme immediately brings to mind Paul's challenge to Timothy to 'do the work of an evangelist; fulfil your ministry' (2 Tim. 4:5 R.S.V.). The clear implication of this passage is that a pastor cannot fulfil his ministry unless he fulfils his role as evangelist. Now certainly this means far more than merely preaching evangelistic sermons from time to time, although that is a part of it. In the light of the Scriptures and in a day like today it *must* mean leading the whole church to become an evangelistic and mission-minded body. And experience has surely taught us, as C. E. Autry puts it:

> The place of the pastor in the evangelism of the local church is strategic. If he is evangelistic, the church will ordinarily be evangelistic. The degree to which the pastor is evangelistic will be reflected in the church. If he is lukewarm, the church will very likely be lukewarm. If he is intensely evangelistic, the church will reflect the warmth and concern of the pastor.[15]

It is evident that a local church eventually takes on the basic attitudes of its pastor. Yet this is as it should be if one's ministry is at all effective. Therefore, I cannot express too forcefully this essential principle of the minister becoming in a true sense a pastor-evangelist. Actually, this is the theme of the entire book, for if a local church is to be an evangelistic church and geared to effective outreach, the pastor is normally the key man to so lead it.

The principle of the pastor-evangelist
But is this really the pastor's role? Is this to overstate

the case? Perhaps we can find an answer to these questions in what the New Testament presents as the position of the pastor in a local congregation. Initially, let it be recognised that today in all of our denominations we are probably not duplicating exactly the New Testament pattern concerning the ministry. No doubt, for example, there was a plurality of elders or pastors which few contemporary churches have. And probably the bishop had a somewhat different role than the present-day bishop in those communions which still keep the office. The point is, however, that the New Testament words which are used to describe the various offices in the first-century Church give us something of an insight into what the function of today's pastor is to be.

Take first, therefore, the word 'presbyters' or 'elders'. This term is essentially a term of dignity. Actually, the Church originally borrowed it from the Jewish community. Members of the Sanhedrin, for example, were often called elders. And it seems clear that the Greeks used the term in a similar fashion before the Jews brought it into their vocabulary. Now the actual *function* of the dignified office of elder is found in the word *episkopoi* or 'bishop', which literally means 'overseer'. Thayer points out: '. . . that they (the elders) did not differ at all from the (*episkopoi*) bishop or overseer (as is acknowledged also by Jerome on Titus 1:5) . . . is evident from the fact that the two words are used indiscriminately. . . . The title *episkopos* denotes the function, *presbuteros* the dignity . . .'[16]

These men were, as the terms imply, essentially the governing body of the Church. They were charged with the task of leading the Church into its proper life and ministry. Paul tells them the Holy Spirit had made them overseers (Acts 20:28) and they were to 'shepherd' (*poimainein*) the Church of God. But this office was not only one of authority—though it was that. In James we find them visiting and praying for the sick (James 5:13-15). In 1 Timothy 5:17 the elders are to 'labour

31

in the word and teaching'. Hebrews 13:7, 17, 24 (while another Greek word is used for the office of elder) states that those who rule are those who 'spake the word of God' and for the sake of the readers 'watch on behalf of their souls'. This combination of ruling with preaching, teaching and pastoral responsibility is clearly in line with the entire New Testament concept of the ministry. Most keenly to be felt by the ministers was their responsibility to God for the welfare of the flock under their charge.

Another aspect of ministry is found in the Greek word *diakonoi* or 'deacon'. Although there no doubt seems to be a special group in the New Testament churches who were appointed to this particular office of ministry, the word is used at times interchangeably with the offices of elder, evangelist, or even apostle (e.g. 1 Cor. 3:5). It is well known that the word essentially means 'service' or 'ministering'. And, as we find again in Thayer, it is often used in connection with those who, by God's command, promote and proclaim religion among men.[17] The prime impact of this word as it relates to the pastor, therefore, is that he is God's servant, ministering to God's people to promote the true faith of Christ.

One of the most interesting passages concerning the ministry in the New Testament Church is that found in Ephesians 4:11-12: 'And these were his gifts: some to be apostles, some prophets, some evangelists, some pastors and teachers to equip God's people for work in his service, to the building up of the body of Christ' (N.E.B.).

These verses clearly present the office-bearers of the first-century Church. It is of interest initially, because it gives us something of an insight into the organisation and administrative structure of the early Church. Barclay states from this Ephesian passage that there were actually three kinds of office-bearers in Paul's time. (1) There were those whose authority and word were universal, i.e. to the entire Church. (2) There were also those whose ministry was not restricted to one place. They had a wandering or itinerant ministry. (3) Finally, there were those who ministered essentially to one congregation in one place.[18]

In the first category of ministry we find the apostles. And this meant more than just the Twelve. For instance, Silvanus (1 Thess. 2:6), Andronicus and Junia (Rom. 16:7) and, of course, Paul and Barnabas were all called apostles in the sense that the term is used in Ephesians 4. It was required that these men had seen the Lord and been a witness to His resurrection. In this historical sense, therefore, this specific office was to pass away. Yet, in the spirit of the office, all true ministers are apostles, for surely they are to be the ones sent (*apostolos*) by God to bear witness to the resurrection, as the term itself implies.

The second group of ministers, the wanderers, are called prophets and evangelists. The prophet, as a forthteller (more than a fore-teller) of God's truth, went about preaching in the power of the Spirit and was a man of great influence. Before long, however, this office seemed to vanish from the life of the early Church. Perhaps there were those who abused the office so that it fell into some disrepute. The evangelists were what we would probably call today missionaries. They were the bringers of good news. They did not exercise the prestige or authority of the apostles; they did not have the early influence of the Spirit-inspired prophets; they were more or less the rank and file missionaries of the Church who went about proclaiming the gospel.

Finally, there were the pastors and teachers. They were the more settled and permanent ministry in the local church. This title that Paul gives to these men seems to be a double phrase to describe one essential group of ministers. Their task is to be seen in their title; they were to teach and preach, and the content of their message was the Christian faith. But these men were more than simply teachers and preachers, they were also pastors (*poi-*

menas) or 'shepherds'. They were to feed the flock of God (1 Pet. 5:2) and to care for and protect the sheep (Acts 20:28). And Jesus Christ Himself is the supreme example, for He is called the Chief Shepherd (1 Pet. 5:4) and the Shepherd of all men's souls (1 Pet. 2:25). What a responsible position this was! As Barclay says, 'The shepherd of the flock of God is the man who bears God's people on his heart, who feeds them with the truth, who seeks them when they stray away, and who defends them from all that would hurt or destroy or distort their faith.'[19]

The impact of this Ephesian passage for our present purpose, however, is not just to give us a picture of the New Testament structures of the ministry, interesting as that is. What is to be seen at the moment is that God gave these gifted men as His gifts to the Church so that the Church might be equipped to do the work of the ministry. As has already been emphasised, it is the whole Church to whom the work of the ministry has been committed. The 'ministers' or 'clergymen' as we commonly call them, are given to the Church to prepare the Church to carry on its ministry. Now the impact of this well-known and much discussed principle in the field of evangelism is obvious. Having discovered that the prime ministry of the Church is mission, the clear implication is that the real evangelists are the church members themselves. And the pastor, therefore, is to equip the Christians under his charge for this vital task. This is surely the only conclusion that can be drawn from all that the New Testament says concerning the leader of a congregation and the role he is to fill relative to mission. He is a bishop, an overseer; he is an elder, a man of respect and honour; he is a deacon, a servant of the people; he is a pastor, one who feeds and guards the flock; he is a preacher and teacher to communicate the faith; he is an apostle, one sent by God; he is a prophet, one who speaks in the power of the Holy Spirit; he is an evangelist, one who heralds good news. This is something of the spirit of the pastor's role as he attempts to lead with spiritual authority his flock into fields of evangelistic ministry. Of course, this is a fantastic order and no man can possibly possess all of these gifts to perfection. Yet it is surely implied that the pastor of a local congregation *must* assume the responsibility of leading and equipping the whole church to fulfil its ministry. It is to this position he has been called by the Holy Spirit. And regardless of how inadequate he may feel—or actually be—to this work he must unreservedly give himself.

So here we are back to the previous theme: the entire Church becoming mobilised and equipped for evangelising our revolutionary society. And I would trust now it is amply clear that the essential responsibility for this Herculean task of leading and equipping the Church settles essentially on the shoulders of the pastor. Surely, this is the most vital aspect of what it means to be a pastor-evangelist. As stated by Whitesell:

> The Pastor-evangelist, then, is the key-man in local church evangelism, and local church evangelism is the key to all other evangelism. The pastor must lead his people in intercessory prayer for the lost; he must inspire them, teach them, organise them, send them out, and encourage them to continue in this greatest of all church work.[20]

This then is the pastor's task, and I think it not put too strongly to say that if he fails in this obligation, he has missed a very vital aspect of his ministry.

Some examples of pastor-evangelists
History is not without its examples to reinforce the validity of this principle. Take, for instance, the marvellous ministry of Richard Baxter of Kidderminster. Although he was pastor in a small town of only 5,000 and came to a very provincial and weak church, he was

soon used to kindle a bright flame of evangelism. It is true he was an exceptionally powerful preacher; he 'preached as a dying man to dying men', he said. It is also true that he did much personal evangelism himself in that he had every family in the community into his home. But these things were not the only reason for the effectiveness of his evangelistic ministry. Perhaps his greatest genius lay in the fact that he led his people to set up family worship in their homes where they themselves could communicate the Christian faith to their families and others. At any rate, as a result of the remarkable work of Baxter as a pastor-evangelist, it has been said that through his ministry 'Kidderminster became a veritable colony of heaven in an hour of general spiritual darkness and wickedness'.[21]

Or take the ministry of Charles Haddon Spurgeon. Granted, he served in a different context than today: people would come by droves to hear a good preacher. Still, he devoted a large part of his ministry to the training of young men to go out and reach those without Christ. Spurgeon said on one occasion, 'He who converts a soul draws water from a fountain, but he who trains a soul-winner digs a well, from which thousands may drink to eternal life.' And space precludes the interesting accounts of men of God who spent much time training 'evangelists' to declare Christ: men like John Wesley, Charles Finney, Bernard of Clairvaux, Francis of Assisi.

But it is when we come to the contemporary scene that we can find perhaps even clearer examples of the principle of the pastor-evangelist at work. I have a personal friend who has excelled in his responsibility in this field.[22] He started his work with two concerned laymen. He taught and encouraged them in the area of personal evangelism. These two men began to lead people to faith in Christ. Soon they recruited two more to join them in the work. Now four men were engaged. This continuing type of growth ensued. Before long women were inspired and they, along with several young people, gave themselves to the task. Now a host of trained and zealous Christians are constantly witnessing. All the organisations of the church, the Sunday School, training classes, women's and men's work, etc., have been caught up in the spirit of mission. The whole church actually throbs with evangelistic fervour. The consequences are that literally hundreds are reached for Christ and His Church every year. It took time, to be sure. There were painful days, and there are still problems. But here was a pastor who saw his role, took it seriously, and starting with only two men and working and training for mission, became a pastor-evangelist in a most profound sense.

Another modern-day example can be seen in the marvellous training and equipping programme of a leading church in the very heart of London.[23] Here the minister faithfully trains large numbers of Christians to serve in the varied programmes of outreach the church has devised. The training is not easy, but people devote themselves to it. And they become effective in reaching others for Christ. Witness to the success of this principle is in the fact that in the centre of a great secular city here is a church with a large congregation every Sunday morning and evening while many other churches are happy to see their buildings half full. Although these factors are not the only means of judging success in God's work, it surely should say something to us if we are honest and open to what God by His Spirit is doing through the ministries of men who have seen and attempted to implement the principle of the pastor-evangelist.

Now it may seem such an impossible task to challenge and mobilise an entire congregation that one despairs of even beginning. And I suppose that the ideal never will be perfectly realised. But regardless of the problems, the principle remains and the obligation must be faced by pastors. Moreover, in Chapter 3 we shall be discussing this theme in far more detail and attempt to present some practical ideas wherein a beginning can perhaps be found. Be that as it may, the inevitable conclusion of all that has been said is quite simple logic. The major premise is that the evangelisation of the turbulent, changing world rests upon the gearing and equipping of the whole Body of Christ to engage in the *missio Dei*. The minor premise is that this mobilisation and equipping task is essentially the responsibility of the pastor in the local congregation. The conclusion can only be that if the mission is significantly successful the pastor must rise to the challenge of his role. If he fails to do so and refuses to become in a very profound sense a pastor-evangelist, the Church seriously suffers. But if he does accept his place in the economy of God, I am convinced the Church can rise from her slumbers and pick up the challenge. This is the counter-revolution I am calling for. And if the challenge is met, the last decades of this century could well see a new and relevant thrust for evangelism that it has not seen for many years.

1. Francis Schaeffer, *The God Who Is There* (London, Hodder and Stoughton, 1968), p. 15.

2. ibid., p. 14.

3. Harvey Cox, *The Secular City* (New York, the Macmillan Company, 1965), p. 35 (London, Penguin, 1968).

4. ibid., p. 2.

5. G. Paul Musselman, 'Evangelism and the Disinherited', from *Evangelism and Contemporary Issues*, edited by Gordon Pratt Baker (Nashville, Tidings Press, 1964), p. 100.

6. Georgia Harkness, 'Evangelism and Secularism', from *Evangelism and Contemporary Issues*, p. 71.

7. Bryan Green, *The Practice of Evangelism* (New York, Charles Scribner's Sons, 1951), p. 16 (London, Hodder and Stoughton, 1951).

8. W. E. Sangster, *Let Me Commend* (Nashville, Abingdon Press, 1948), p. 14 (London, Hodder and Stoughton, 1949; Wyvern Books, 1961).

9. S. Paul Schilling, 'The Meaning of Evangelism', from *Evangelism and Contemporary Issues*, p. 9.

10. Douglas Webster, *What is Evangelism?* (London, The Highway Press, 1964), p. 105.

11. Robert Beach Cunningham, 'Evangelism and the Challenge of the City', from *Evangelism and Contemporary Issues*, p. 94.

12. Faris Daniel Whitesell, *Basic New Testament Evangelism* (Grand Rapids, Zondervan, 1949), p. 133.

13. Leighton Ford, *The Christian Persuader* (New York, Harper and Row, 1966), p. 45 (London, Hodder and Stoughton, 1967).

14. *The Church for Others* (Geneva, World Council of Churches, 1968), pp. 18–19.

15. C. E. Autrey, *Basic Evangelism* (Grand Rapids, Zondervan, 1954), p. 63.

16. Jospeh Henry Thayer, *A Greek-English Lexicon of the New Testament* (New York, American Book Company, 1886), p. 536. H. J. Carpenter in *A Theological Wordbook of the Bible* holds that only some in the body of elders in a church would have the function of *episkopoi* (p. 150).

17. ibid., p. 137.

18. William Barclay, *The Letters to the Galatians and Ephesians* in the Daily Study Bible Series (Philadelphia, Westminster Press, 1956), pp. 171 ff. (Edinburgh, St Andrew Press, 1954).

19. ibid., p. 175.

20. Faris Daniel Whitesell, op. cit., p. 144.

21. C. E. Autrey, op. cit., p. 66.

22. Rev. John Turpin, former pastor of the Beth Haven Baptist Church, Louisville, Kentucky.

23. All Souls' Church (Church of England), the Rev. John Stott, Rector.

2

A Theology of Evangelism

If the Church would effectively evangelise today it must do so from a strong theological base. It has been quite correctly stated that 'There can be no effective and permanent evangelism without theology, and there would soon be few persons ready to study theology without evangelism'.[1] If evangelism loses sight of theology, it does so at its own peril. And theology divorced from the fervour of evangelism is dry and tasteless. It cannot be stated too strongly that the two disciplines, if ever severed, part to their mutual detriment.

Reasons for uniting theology and evangelism
There are very sound reasons why theology and mission must not be separated. The first and by far the most important reason is that they are never divorced in the Scriptures. This is evident, by the simple fact that the books of the New Testament were not composed primarily as dissertations on Christian theology; rather, they were the 'incidental literature of evangelism'.[2] It is clear, for example, that many of Paul's most profound doctrinal statements grew out of an evangelistic and pastoral concern for the churches. But obviously they do at the same time give us in unsystematic form the very essence of our Christian theology. Yet all of this stands to reason, for evangelism by its very name implies a theology. It is the good *news* that God has revealed

about Himself. Thus it can be put in propositional form. It can be discussed. Its implications can be formulated. And this is theology. So the evangelistic passion grows out of doctrinal sources. From the purely biblical perspective the two go hand in glove.

A second reason for the wedding of theology and mission is that without sound theological content, evangelism soon degenerates into sentimentalism, emotionalism and gimmicks. Such charges have at times been directed towards the evangelistically minded. Moreover, there is all too often substance to the criticisms. And it is rather dishonest—and may even betray a simple laziness—for the Evangelical to retort that such a charge grows out of spiritual coldness and a lack of concern for the unbelieving world. Any form of evangelism that resorts to the manipulation of people, regardless of the motive, is unworthy of the gospel. More tragically, such an experience can lead unsuspecting and honest inquirers into a shallow experience that falls short of a genuine experience of salvation. Scriptural evangelism demands that the evangelist fills his presentation of the gospel with solid theological content. It is a price that must be paid if God's approval on the work is expected, for people are rarely genuinely converted to faith in Christ by psychological manœuvring, persuasive oratory or emotional stories. For the sake of those whom we would reach for Christ, authentic theology and evangelism must not be severed.

Finally, the third reason for fusing theology and evangelism is because of the pragmatic fact that God has honoured most profoundly the ministry of those who do. A mere cursory survey of the history of mission demonstrates this clearly. The early Church fathers are a patent instance. Augustine of Hippo in the fourth and fifth centuries was a great theologian. His system of thought was foundational not only in his own day, but it also had significant influence on the reformers a millennium later. Yet he was also a very effective evangelist.

His great work *The City of God* was inspired directly by the spirit of mission. Concerning Christian theology, Augustine said it 'must be carried into practice, and . . . taught for the very purpose of being practised . . .'; the preacher must 'sway the mind so as to subdue the will'. Thus he implemented in his ministry that beautiful blend of theology and evangelism. And illustrations of this type can be multiplied over again. One thinks of men like Calvin, Luther, Arminius, Wesley and Whitefield. In more recent times the principle is seen in men like Charles Finney, the great American evangelist of the nineteenth century whose ministry won thousands and who, at the same time, taught theology at Oberlin College for over forty years. R. A. Torrey, a very successful evangelist, was such a student that he read his polyglot Bible every day. And a number of our own contemporaries could be stated. Thus one can conclude from a purely practical perspective that God uses the man most significantly who sees and injects into his evangelistic service a sound theology. Simply put, 'Theology is to evangelism what the skeleton is to the body. Remove the skeleton and the body becomes a helpless quivering mass of jelly-like substance. By means of the skeleton the body can stand erect and move. The great systems of theological truths form the skeleton which enables our revealed religion to stand.'[3]

There are further reasons that could be elaborated upon as to the necessity of a strong theology for effective evangelism. For example, a knowledge of theology makes the presentation of the gospel message plain; it makes the evangelist more sure of his message; a genuine understanding of the rich content of the Bible will fill one with zeal; theology is an important agent in conserving evangelistic results. But the above three reasons should surely convince any Christian who seeks to win the unbeliever that theology and mission must be forever united.

Therefore the pastor-evangelist must formulate a

strong theology of evangelism. Obviously, space will preclude any attempt to present a thorough-going doctrinal statement of mission. It may even appear a bit presumptuous to give only one chapter to a theme that can boast volumes. Yet there are basic truths one must make ingredient to his life if he is to be effective in mission activity. So we shall be brave and briefly discuss these aspects of theology so as to present at least a working outline.

The necessity of conversion

It seems obvious that the biblical presentation of the necessity of conversion is the first foundation stone in developing a theology of evangelism. It may appear to some as quite unnecessary even to approach such an obvious fact. Yet today this truth is implicitly, if not explicitly, being more and more called into question. The growing spirit of syncretism and universalism is being felt even in circles that have been traditionally evangelical and evangelistic. Especially is this true among younger, educated people. Thus it seems appropriate to approach the subject.

The necessity of conversion, of course, rests on the scriptural doctrine of man and the fall. As has often been said, to understand the good news of God we must first understand the bad news of man.[4] Appropriately, therefore, in the early chapters of Genesis we have the account of the creation of man, his corruption by sin and the consequences of his wilful disobedience. The Bible thereafter uses several figures to describe man in his rebellious state. He is seen as fallen, corrupted, blind, diseased, lost, dead, etc. These ideas are all efforts to portray the fact that something is terribly awry with human character. The Bible sees man's very nature and personhood as severely perverted. There is absolutely no scriptural warrant for holding the view that man is essentially good, even despite the fact that he was created in God's image. Man stands in desperate need. He is in

44

real trouble. But where is this trouble rooted? Ruten-ber has correctly said it lies in an utter 'failure of re-lationships'.[5]

Man is never just an object. He is not an atomic sim-ple. He is not 'just there'. Man can never be understood apart from his basic relationships. These essential rela-tionships, Rutenber tells us, are three: (a) his relation to God; (b) his relation to his fellows; and (c) his relation to himself. He is related to God in that he is made for fellowship with God. This is the meaning of the *Deo imageo*. He is made in and for the love of God. This makes him responsible and human. Secondly, he is re-lated to his fellows in a social sense. No man can be 'an island entire to himself'. Inter-human relationships are a vital part of that which makes life what it is. Finally, man is related to himself, i.e. he can talk to himself, he can think about himself; in a word, he has self-conscious-ness. Moreover, he can have a hand in the forging of his own character and personality.

Sin corrupts life's relationships
Now, when man became disobedient to God, all of his basic relationships were corrupted. Sin bludgeoned almost to death every important tie that makes life worth living. First, sin in the human-divine relationship means guilt. And it is genuine guilt, not just neurotic guilt feelings. Sin is a refusal by man to let God act in his life, i.e. to be God in a real sense. And this makes one truly guilty before God. Of course, guilt feelings arise. They should do—man is guilty. He is culpable. He stands condemned. Judgment—eternal judgment—is his lot, for the essential God-man relationship is broken.

In the second place, sin in relation to one's fellows results in lovelessness. The only thing that holds the structures of society together in true harmony is love. When love degenerates, society with its vital human relationships also crumbles. Little wonder that the world is in the condition it is! With love gone, only selfishness remains, even if it is very cultured or restrained by law.

Finally, sin in relation to one's own self means bondage, perversion, frustration and depression. Self relatedness is corrupted by evil just as surely as are the other essential relationships of life. One can only 'be himself' when properly related to God. As Rutenber graphically describes it: 'With God lost, I am thrown back on myself to live off my own nerves and feed off my own fingernails.'[6] Summarily stated, sin perverts all of life; man is guilty, loveless and in bondage.

Though sin and the fall means more, perhaps much more, it should at least be clear that man stands in desperate need of change. Moreover, a little straightening up here and there will never do. He stands in need of radical, revolutionary change. He needs to become a whole new man. His entire system of relationships cries out to be altered. He needs reconciliation at a profound depth. He needs to die and start over again. And that is just what conversion means. It is the 'turn' that utterly transforms life. That is why we contend vigorously for the absolute necessity of conversion.

Now the fact of man's need is the rationale behind the scriptural call to repentance and faith, for this is what brings about a true conversion experience. And the Bible is unmistakably clear in its demands for such an exercise of will. As Michael Green, in his excellent work *Evangelism in the Early Church*, has said:

> . . . although it [salvation] is absolutely universal in its offer, Mark knows that the good news is only effective among those who repent, believe, and are prepared to engage in costly, self-sacrificial discipleship. Only the man who is prepared to lose his life for the sake of Christ and the gospel can find it; for it was only in losing his life for the sake of others that Christ could offer new life to men, the new life proclaimed in the gospel.[7]

In the light of these truths it strikes one as a bit of a mystery why some seemingly desire to downgrade the inescapable necessity of a conversion experience. Perhaps it grows out of a misunderstanding of the nature or message of the Bible or a shallow grasp of the real condition of man. Moreover, at the same time, I do not suppose that many Evangelicals themselves will be very zealous in their evangelistic labours until they are utterly convinced of these facts and begin to feel the compassion of Christ concerning the depth of man's plight. This is surely vital to a dynamic theology of evangelism.

God as Redeemer
This then leads us to see what God has done to remedy man's awful sickness. As we have seen, the Scriptures paint a dark and sombre picture of man's sin. But they also paint a bright portrait of God as the Redeemer and Reconciler of man. In a word, the whole Bible is saying: God redeems.

God redeems as Father. He desires men to become His sons, so He sent His Son. He reveals Himself as Father, so He desires that we live in that relationship. He is King, so He wishes men to submit to that authority. He is the giver of life, so He wants all to receive its fullness. Above all, He is love, and so He pleads with us to receive that love and walk in a fellowship of love with Him.

God redeems as Son. This is obvious. The good news *is* the news about the Son, and the entire Christ event is all about redemption. This is the essence of the incarnation; it was what He did as man that made it possible for Him to do anything for man. The cross is all redemption, from the first blow of the hammer that pierced His hand until the cry 'It is finished'. 'In my place condemned He stood. Sealed my pardon with His blood. Hallelujah! What a Saviour.' Further, the resurrection means a redeemed life. The Christian experience is a perpetual Easter. Little wonder Paul wrote, 'We preach Christ'.

God redeems as Holy Spirit. It is He who convinces of sin, righteousness and judgment (John 16:7–11). It is He who inspires faith. It is He who is the agent in the regeneration experience (John 3:5, 8). It is He who seals the new-born Christian (Eph. 1:3). It is He who comes to abide as God in the human life and thus makes the human body the temple of God (1 Cor. 6:19). It is He who makes the believer truly different by 'forming Christ within' (Gal. 4:19). Apart from the working of the Holy Spirit, there is no personal redemption. The Holy Spirit makes the saving Christ one's constant contemporary. All the triune Godhead is thus involved in man's reconciliation.

Now concerning the atonement that God has accomplished in Christ we should perhaps give it a bit more detailed attention. It is essential to a sound theology of mission that one has something of a grasp of the meaning of the atonement, for from this develops that confidence in the reconciling work of Jesus Christ that will motivate one to proclaim fearlessly its tremendous truths.

The necessity of confidence in the atonement of Christ
There was a time when much interest was shown in the various theories of the atonement. It was then the exercise of most theologians to elucidate in some detail each concept and then discuss at length its various merits and defects. Space, if not contemporary interest, forbids such a detailed exercise here. Yet, it may still be helpful to see at least the salient contribution the different theories have given to our understanding of the work of Christ. It is somewhat difficult to classify the various ideas of atonement, but the following may suffice.

Theories of the atonement
    The Governmental (Grotion) Theory. This concept of the atonement, recently defended by A. B. Crabtree,

tells us that Christ was essentially a substitute for us. He stood in our place and bore our penalty. It sees the atonement as a satisfaction but not as an internal principle of the divine nature. This, of course, is its weakness. Still, it is true that the law and its demands had to be met. And Christ accomplished this when He died in our place and bore our judgment in Himself. Here is one aspect of the truth to be fully understood and forthrightly proclaimed in the presentation of the gospel. We are pardoned because Christ bore our punishment.

The Example (Socinian) Theory. This view of the atonement states that by Christ's example, man is motivated to reconcile himself to God. Of course, the weakness of this approach, as its very name implies, rests in its failure to grasp the fact that God must also be seen as reconciled to man in the work of Christ as well as the converse. Dr Vincent has apparently grasped this truth when he speaks of God's 'transformed face' towards sinners. But the theory does point out at least, and quite correctly, that man desperately needs reconciling to God, i.e. that the basic divine-human relationship must be restored. Further, it has seen that the death of Christ is a tremendous example of faithfulness to truth and duty and thus has a powerful influence on one's own moral improvement. Christ's example of love and sacrifice should kindle a similar love in us. Of course, the cross is far more than example, yet it surely is that also. Incidentally, the so-called Bushnelian or moral influence theory has much the same approach with its attending failings and strong points.

The Commercial (Anselmic) Theory. The impact of this conception of the atoning work of Christ rests in its grasp of the fact that the divine honour was grossly sinned against in the fall. The consequences are that infinite punishment must attend the offender. As can be deduced, it suffers from a lack of understanding that more than the divine honour was at stake in the fall. Moreover, the atonement of Calvary did far more than meet in an *exact equivalent* the divine claims, as this theory implies. The work of Christ on the cross was not that formal and external. And surely the divine honour cannot become more prominent than divine holiness. Yet one must grant that God's honour was involved in it all and in that sense the concept has something to say.

The Dramatic (Patristic) Theory. Here the emphasis is on the struggle between the forces of God and the forces of evil. In one sense, this tends to leave man somewhat out of the picture in its stress on the struggle of opposing forces. And surely man was deeply involved in the whole affair. At the same time, however, it is clear that a great battle was being waged and the forces of evil were routed and destroyed in the Christ event.

The Ransom Theory. This is also sometimes called the patristic view. Further, it is something of a variation of the above concept. The idea is that if we were redeemed through a ransom paid by God, the one who was paid must have been Satan. Few, if any, hold such a morally repugnant view today; although Aulen, in his *Christus Victor*, proposes something of a demythologised view of the concept. Of course, it is true that our salvation was very costly to God. But He hardly paid a ransom for captive men to the Devil or anyone. The truth to be stressed in the concept of a ransom paid is that the atonement price was the costly blood of Christ, and God who paid that price is thus the great deliverer. We shall expand this in more detail when later in this chapter we consider the idea of justification.

The Ethical Theory. A. H. Strong seemingly attempts to bring together the strengths of these other views in the approach he conceived and called the Ethical Theory. He makes the following points: (a) the atonement must be seen as rooted in the holiness of God. (b) it must answer the ethical demands of the divine nature. (c) in the humanity of Christ and His sufferings all claims of justice are met. (d) Christ suffered vicariously. (e) the atonement was accomplished through the solidarity of the race. (f) it satisfies man's ethical needs. (g) the atonement is for all, but man must avail himself of it.

Now whether or not we agree with all Strong asks for, it seems he has grasped the importance of gleaning from the various theories that aspect of the truth they present and then incorporating them into a full system. This approach has obvious value, for the atonement is a many-faceted jewel. To fix one's gaze upon just one facet is to neglect the beauty of the whole. Actually, so profound is the scriptural presentation of the atonement that a completely satisfying theology is most difficult, if not impossible. The more we look into its wonders, the more glorious it becomes. But we must continue our gaze and continue to pass on to others what wonders we discover.

Of course there are other, modern, quite unique interpretations of the atonement. These are of great interest but must be left for more critical studies. Now perhaps a brief excursion into some of the various biblical words that describe salvation will help us most in gaining deeper understanding and more profound confidence in the atonement of Christ.

The biblical meaning of salvation

A term we have already used several times is the word 'conversion'. The New Testament word-group is based on the Greek noun *epistrephein*. As could be expected, this group is used in classical and *koine* Greek in a non-theological sense. It means simply 'to turn' as to turn a ship or turn around. It can also connote 'to turn the mind' or 'turn one's attention to'. Etymologically this led in the usage of the word to mean 'to warn', 'to correct', 'to cause to repent'. Thus we see it acquiring religious overtones. Quite naturally, therefore, the New Testament writers picked it up. It was ideally suited to present the concept behind conversion. In the Scriptures themselves the word-group in its substantial and verbal forms is used some thirty-five times. It is rarely used in a transitive sense except in Luke 1:16–17 and James 5:19–20. It is frequently used in a physical sense of turning or returning, e.g. Matt. 12:44, Luke 2:39, etc. But for our immediate interest, it is most often employed to connote a mental or spiritual turn. Classic examples are Peter's call to repentance in Acts 3:19 and the account of Acts 9:35 where many 'turned' to the Lord. The Old Testament equivalent *shubh* occurs some 1,146 times and is used in much the same fashion as the *epistrephein* word-group. The basic theological idea is this: one is called to turn, to change the direction of his thinking, affections, willing, etc. It implies a complete reversal of all of life. Now this would indicate that he turns *from* something *to* something. And such it is; he turns from himself to God. As Brunner has expressed it, repentance is coming alive to one's true self as a sinner and faith is coming to God as a Saviour. This is conversion.

'Redemption' is a very common word in current theological writings. This wide use of the term is a relatively modern development, however. It is used sparsely in the New Testament, and theologians normally followed that pattern until quite recent times. When the word was employed by older writers, it was used in a much more restricted sense. Of course, the man in the street of the first century thought of it in a completely non-religious sense as is the case with so many of the terms that now have deep theological implications. The basic word is *lutron*, i.e. ransom. The term is derived from *luō*, meaning to loose. It was used to describe almost any kind of loosing, like the loosing of men from prison. However, when one was loosed as a prisoner of war, a ransom price was paid. Hence the concept of release on receipt of ransom grew up around the term. Thus, as Morris points out, 'this idea of payment as the basis of release . . . is the reason for the existence of the whole word-group'.[8] The Hebrew equivalents are : (a) $g'l$ where only Yahweh is used as the subject of the verbal forms; (b) *pah* where the idea is of a ransom acquired by the payment of a price; and (c) *kopher* which means the actual ransom price itself.

So we can see that the basic concept in redemption is the paying of a ransom price to secure a liberation. When God is the subject of the verb, however, there is a shift of emphasis. It is not conceivable, as Morris correctly states, that God could pay a ransom to man, and surely not to the Devil as the old ransom theory of the atonement tries to tell us. Therefore, the stress must be placed upon the idea of deliverance rather than on the means by which it is brought about. At the same time, however, the thought is there that God delivers his people at a cost—and at a high cost. We know of course what that cost was, namely, the precious blood of Christ (1 Pet. 1 : 18–19). Consequently, 'Believers are not brought by Christ into a liberty of selfish ease. Rather, since they have been bought by God at terrible cost, they have become God's slaves, to do His will'.[9] A proper understanding and declaration of this tremendous truth should surely help save us from a shallow evangelism.

It would appear that the dominating idea in Paul's concept of salvation is found in the word 'justification'. At any rate, this is true if one can judge from the sheer number of times he employs the thought. The word-group from which this term derives is *dikaios*, i.e. 'righteous'. The basic concept that centres around this theme is of a proper standing before God. It is a status of righteousness conferred on men by God upon the basis of the work of Christ in His death and resurrection. Emphasis must be laid on the idea of imputation, for there is no sense in which such a status can be attained by human works of righteousness. The roots of the doctrine are found in the Old Testament view of righteousness, and Morris contends it is vital to realise this to appreciate the New Testament meaning of salvation. God in His holiness demands righteousness among men. This the Law clearly demonstrates. But as the first-century Jew probably saw this as performing deeds of legal righteousness, the New Testament believer sees it as an *imputed* righteousness. For man is a sinner and cannot be righteous in himself. But Christ died for all and fulfilled the demands of the Law in our stead. Classical Protestantism has thus interpreted the whole idea as to mean that Christ endured the penalty of sin and in this way demonstrated that the eternal law of righteousness cannot be disputed. As Calvin put it, 'As the law allowed no remission, and God did remit sins, there appeared to be a stain on divine justice. The exhibition of Christ as an atonement is what alone removes it.'[10]

So a man is justified, made righteous in God's sight, when he exercises faith in the atoning work of Christ. Faith opens up to him this new status. The forensic implications of the entire concept stand out clearly and must be made plain. Lenski holds that *dikaios* is *always* forensic. Perhaps this truth has special meaning and relevance to our so-called lawless society.

It may well be, however, that the most relevant aspect of salvation to our day centres in the truths implied by the word 'reconciliation'. We have already pointed out in some detail that man lives in a three-fold relationship, i.e. to God, his fellows and himself. And it is the rupturing of these vital relationships that comprises the tragedy of sin. Man, in rebellion towards God, is guilty, loveless and experiences an inner bondage. Reconciliation means the restoring of these essential and vital relationships.

Rutenber interestingly points out that modern psychiatry is deeply involved with these three problems in man. But it is clear that the psychiatrist deals with them on an entirely different level. Still, the problems of guilt, inability to give and/or receive love and lack of freedom to function properly in society occupies the counsellor constantly. But though the psychiatrist may remove neurotic guilt, real guilt remains; and though he may enable a loveless neurotic to give and receive love on a human level, only Christ can impart by his Holy Spirit the *agape* love of God; and though the doctor may help a man find release from fear so as to function more successfully as a useful member of society, only the new birth gives one the true liberty of the sons of God. In other words, 'psychiatry and the gospel work on a man's problems on different though not unrelated levels. The well-integrated, well adjusted, and socially well-manicured person still needs redemption.'[11]

But the preoccupation of the contemporary psychiatrist with these problems demonstrates the desperate need of man for reconciliation. And it is just that which Christ's salvation provides. First, one is reconciled to God, for salvation means forgiveness—real forgiveness for real sin. God freely pardons us in Christ. This forgiveness reaches much deeper than just neurotic guilt feelings. True guilt before God and its attending feelings are eradicated. Thus one can say with Paul, 'We have peace with God through our Lord Jesus Christ' (Rom. 5:1). Moreover, through Christ's work in death and resurrection, God is genuinely reconciled to man. This is a theological truth not to be overlooked or ignored. Reconciliation is a two-way street. Consequently, the sinner recognises God's moral prerogative to forgive justly in Christ. For before forgiveness becomes *morally* effective, the conscience and moral sense of the forgiven must be satisfied. And Christ completely meets these demands and Christian reconciliation with its marvellous peace is met on this double level of depth. The forgiven sinner knows God has not 'leaned over backwards' to forgive him. God remains just and yet the justifier of those who believe (Rom. 3:26). Therefore, forgiveness and reconciliation can be offered on a basis that the forgiven one is not humiliated and his self-respect taken away. Moreover, the moral structure of the universe is safeguarded. As Rutenber has reminded us, 'The cross makes forgiveness possible without making righteousness secondary'.[12]

Reconciled to God, man is now free to love his fellows, be reconciled to them and become a reconciling agent. But even the man in Christ cannot love as he should if he relies solely on his humanity. So God sheds his *agape* love abroad in our hearts by the Holy Spirit (Rom. 5:5). Thus in a very real sense, Christ loves through us. The quality of this love is obviously much different from the *eros* love of the world, as Nygren has told us.[13] This *agape* kind of love is an interested love; it demonstrates an infinitely imaginative interest in the well-being of others. It is persistent, continually persistent, in meeting needs. Further, it is not given because the object of love is lovable or fills a vacuum in the life of the lover; that is love on the *eros* level. Rather, it is unconditional. There are no 'ifs' or 'buts' about it. It loves regardless of the response, the character of the one loved, or the reaction of society. Moreover, it is non-sentimental, non-indulgent, mature. It always seeks the best for the other even though it may be quite painful. *Agape* is always vulnerable, open to suffering. In a word, *agape* love is reconciling. It takes the initiative and heals, restores and cures broken lives and relationships because it is completely selfless. This is God's kind of love and the kind of love demonstrated to us in Christ. And with Christ in one's life, this reconciling love is bestowed on others. If these truths are not relevant to today's ruptured society, one wonders what is.

Finally, reconciled to God and one's fellows, man is also reconciled to himself and is free—really free—to function as a mature member of society. We tend to think of our sophisticated culture with its rejection of the old superstitions, taboos and animism of the past as one quite free from fear. That which formerly bound the human personality has now been shown up as false, we are told. Thus man is free from the shackles of fear. We can grow and expand. I wonder! True, we have laid to rest much which should have been buried long ago. But is not the problem that of a basic inner bondage? And though our cultural development and enlightenment has eliminated the old outward manifestations of that bondage, I doubt it has done a great deal to solve the real difficulty, man's estrangement from his true self. Instead of laying our fears to the influence of some evil spirit in a tree as man once did, we now attribute it to some negative experience of childhood or fear of the bomb. Granted, this may be a better diagnosis of the sickness, but what we need is a cure. Man is still in bondage to himself. As Paul put it in Romans, 'I do not understand my own actions. For I do not do what I want, but I do the very thing I hate. I see in my members another law at war with the law of my mind and making me captive . . .' (Rom. 7:1, 5, 23). But in Christ one is truly free. He is freed from that imprisonment to his fallen self; he is free from the fear of the future and the past; his fear of men dissipates; the enslavement of guilt goes; and he can really breathe deeply for the first time. Life takes on meaning. The questions of today's youth: who am I? and where am I going? are satisfyingly answered. He does not have to stand on the corner with Beckett and wait for Godot to come—Godot comes. And he truly does become an 'authentic self'. That is reconciliation, and that is most applicable to today's bewildered, meaningless world.

Thus man stands in the salvation the Godhead provides. Because God is concerned with the whole man, the needs of the whole man are met in the Lord Jesus Christ. Now there are other biblical concepts concerning salvation that space simply forbids us considering, e.g. propitiation, adoption, new creation, covenant, and so on. But perhaps the bare outline of the above aspects of redemption may enable us to begin developing such utter and complete confidence in the atonement of Jesus Christ that we shall herald that good news with a positive joy and enthusiasm.

Confidence in the power of the gospel

This ushers us into a brief consideration of the importance of acquiring confidence in the actual message we are to proclaim. Paul said, 'I am not ashamed of the gospel: it is the power of God for salvation to everyone who has faith' (Rom. 1:16). And such must be our spirit and attitude. The right approach was voiced by C. H. Spurgeon when on a certain occasion a young ministerial student asked him how to defend successfully the gospel. Spurgeon replied, 'How do you defend a lion? You don't, you just turn him loose.' But is one justified in having such confidence in the gospel? The answer is yes, because it is the good news *about* God *from* God. Its source and its content are divine. This is why confidence in the power of the message can be seen as most reasonable to the Christian.

Moreover, the above truths imply that we need not— yea, *must* not—rely on human ingenuity alone, psychological manipulations, dramatics, or any mere human invention, to convince men of the truth and relevance of the message. God will speak for Himself through His word. His Holy Spirit will press home the truth. The gospel truly is 'the power of God unto salvation'.

Furthermore, the gospel speaks to the human situation as no other truth does. Whether or not man will admit his desperate need of reconciliation, that is his actual and deepest need. Consequently, the gospel stands as the most relevant message he can hear. This point we have been labouring. But it is right here that we must be most careful. We *must* present the gospel to the living human situation. We must never simply grind out the truth—even gospel truth. A cold delivery of evangelical orthodoxy is fatal. Just 'delivering a message' can be a 'savour of death unto death' (2 Cor. 2:16). We speak to real people in a real human situation. Their sin is real and concrete. Their fears, frustrations and thwarted ambitions have genuine substance. They are involved in a true social context. They cry for help where they are. What I am trying to say is, it is people that matter. People matter as much as principle. Our Lord's ministry reflected this. He addressed men in their actual living situation. He talked about concrete, contemporary issues. True, He never compromised principle or truth, but it was always addressed in love to people in their personal, immediate needs. Many who are evangelistically minded need to be reminded of this. Some seem so concerned with orthodoxy they forget that truth standing alone is irrelevant if not an outright abstraction. Orthodoxy is important. But it is the orthodox gospel put in the terms of life itself and presented in love to real people that God honours. But more of this later when we take up the problems of communication in today's complex world. Suffice it to say in summary that our message is one of power. It meets the deepest of human needs and we must have utter confidence in it if we are to be effective as the evangelistic Church.

We are co-labourers with God
The fourth essential principle to recognise in a developing theology of evangelism is that expressed by Paul to the Corinthian believers when he said, 'We are God's fellow-workers' (1 Cor. 3:9 margin). The rationale for this principle is found in the truth expressed in Chapter 1 that the mission to evangelise is essentially God's mission, the *missio Dei*. As the working group of the W.C.C. has stated, 'Mission is basically understood as God working out His purpose for His creation, the church does not have a separate mission of its own. It is called to participate in God's mission. The missionary call is a call for participation.'[14]

In other words, in the final analysis, God is the Evangelist. It is essentially God who does the work. This must be kept constantly before the Church. We can so easily get bogged down in the details of either our biblical and theological studies or the practical work of the Church that we miss this one central theme of the Scriptures. I suspect if the Bible were handed to a man who had never seen one before, when he finished reading it, he would probably summarise the entire book by simply saying, 'God is out to redeem me.' This is a truth we must never lose sight of. It will save us from a 'sanctified humanism' that has so often plagued evangelism.

But, as we discussed earlier, there is a parallel truth—perhaps a paradoxical truth—that God never redeems anyone apart from the instrumentality of His people, the Church. This may seem something of an overstatement, yet the Scriptures surely bear it out. Pentecost's thousands came to Christ through the witness of Peter and the Twelve. Cornelius, though addressed by an angel, heard the gospel itself from Simon. Paul, who was actually accosted by the glorified Christ Himself, heard what he was to do from Ananias. And though sent by an angel, it was still Philip who taught the Ethiopian eunuch about Christ. And so through the New Testament and subsequent Church history, the principle persists. In commenting on this truth, Lenski points out, 'Here we see how Jesus honours His ministry. Philip is sent to the eunuch by an angel, it is not the angel who is sent to teach the eunuch. And this is the case wherever the gospel is to be offered.'[15]

Now these principles involve two tremendous implications relative to the Church. First, we can be assured of success because God is with us—or perhaps we should say that we are with God. It is, of course, true that this success cannot be judged by human standards. But if this is God's work in which we are engaged as co-labourers, final success is certain. This should be a great encouragement and a strong stimulus to tireless effort. We are never alone.

Secondly, an awesome responsibility is put on the Church. If God has no other plans for world redemption outside of the use of the agency of His people, the mandate to co-operate with God in His work is very pressing indeed. I think I have already made it clear that I see it as essential to evangelism and the Kingdom that we enthusiastically engage in this work. A short time ago I was preaching along the line of the necessity of Christians becoming witnesses for Christ. Perhaps I was waxing eloquent a bit too much, but I made the statement that unless God's people become enthusiastic witnesses, many will not be converted. After the service, a young lady challenged me on my statement. Surely, she said in effect, those whom God has elected will be converted regardless of what we do. Now I suppose there is a real element of truth on that side of the paradoxical coin of election and freedom. But there is also the other side which declares that God uses his people in his quest for men. And the implications of what will happen if God's people fail in the mission can be legitimately drawn. At least Ezekiel seemed to think so. He tells us :

> So to you, son of man, I have made a watchman for the house of Israel; whenever you hear a word from my mouth, you shall give them warning from me. If I say to the wicked, O wicked man, you shall surely die, and you do not speak to warn the wicked to turn from his way, that wicked man shall die in his iniquity, but his blood I shall require at your hand. But if you warn the wicked to turn from his way, and he does not turn from his way, he shall die in his iniquity, but you will have saved your life. (Ezek. 33 : 7–8)

My interview with the young lady was somewhat reminiscent of Carey's encounter with the old brother who told him to sit down after his plea for missionaries, for if God wanted to convert the heathen he would do it without Carey's help. But we are thankful today that Carey did not sit down but zealously went after men for Christ. And such must be the attitude of the contemporary Church if we take seriously the principle of being co-labourers with God. This to me seems vital for a sound theology of evangelism. The local church as a whole must be motivated to engage in mission and I do not believe it will get so involved unless it gets rooted in a sound understanding of the *missio Dei*.

Finally, in exploring a theology of evangelism, let us look briefly at

The basic biblical principles of evangelistic methodology
This theme could, of course, become a volume in itself. It is therefore quite difficult to attempt to deal with it in a few words. Yet it is vital to see, if only in simplest form, some of these important principles, because evangelistic activity that neglects or ignores biblical methodologies is doomed to failure. Tersely put, we must do God's work in God's way. We shall approach this subject by looking briefly into the ministry of our Lord and then the early Church.

First, note ten salient points from the ministry of Christ.

1. Primarily, Jesus gave of Himself unreservedly; He shared His own personhood on behalf of the needy. Of course, He did this in a fashion we never can. Yet we must surely emulate His principle if we are to be effective as evangelists. This is foundational.

2. He confronted people with the great issues. He was never side-tracked on theological fads. He kept on the main line. Yet He dealt with these great, profound truths with a marvellous simplicity. 'The common people heard Him gladly' (Mark 12:37). The preacher who overshoots his people is not following Jesus's example.

3. He never compromised the demanding claims of the gospel to win followers. He always presented His

absolute Lordship as the cost of discipleship. He never cut corners to gain anyone; the classic case being the rich young ruler.

4. At the same time, He had profound respect for human personality. He never bulldozed anyone. He was always patient, understanding and loving. He was characterised by dignity—and that in a good, mature sense. He never made anyone less of a person, even in His occasional scathing denunciations.

5. He presented the truth uncompromisingly and challenged men to decide then and there. He asked Peter, James and John to choose right then between their nets or discipleship. Matthew was directly and pointedly confronted with the life-deciding issue of whether it would be God or mammon. And he had to decide while he sat right at the bench that was loaded with mammon. There is a principle implied here that many need to grasp today. So often we just leave the gospel for people 'to think over' in such a nebulous way that we rob it of its challenge to immediate commitment. There is the time to wait, to be sure. But there is also the time to call men to decision.

6. It seems evident from the life of our Lord that He had a definite strategy. For example, 'His face was set towards Jerusalem' (Luke 9:53). Jesus knew what He was about and where He was going. To update this principle into modern terms, He had a programme. This, too, we desperately need to learn. But we shall be considering this principle later.

7. He did not attempt to do all the work Himself. He taught, encouraged, nurtured and commissioned His disciples. The implications of this fact are clear and numerous as regards the local church.

8. He was, above all, compassionate. He saw the people as sheep without a shepherd. And no personal sacrifice was ever too great to hinder our Lord from ministering. He was always in the spirit of the towel and basin washing feet. For He said, 'The Son of Man

came not to be served but to serve and to give his life . . .' (Matt. 20:28).

9. He ministered to the whole man. Physical, mental and spiritual needs were met quite indiscriminately by Jesus. Whatever or wherever needs arose, He met them. He knew little of the so-called divisions of secular and sacred, spiritual and physical, saving and social gospel, and so on.

10. Lastly, He saw prayer as the one indispensable exercise in His mission. And how can it be otherwise with us? Thus our Lord ministered His good news and people came by the multitudes to see and hear—and not a few believed.

Let us take a final look at Pentecost as something of a model for local church evangelism. Granted, much more than evangelistic principles is implied by the day of Pentecost. This day was a great epoch in the Church. But surely there is much that can be learned concerning local mission by the events of the day, that is, provided we attempt to do so without doing violence to the other great theological truths of Pentecost and provided we recognise that many of these truths are the most prominent in the scriptural account.

First of all, it is evident that Pentecost is telling us that this is the age of the Spirit. God has not withdrawn from salvation history with the ascension of Jesus Christ. Just the converse is true; He is now in the work as profoundly as when He was in Christ during the days of His flesh. Thus all effective mission is carried on in the context of a Spirit-led, inspired and energised ministry.

Secondly, Pentecost points up the fact that before anything happens significantly in the unbelieving community, something of great significance must happen to the Church. The city of Jerusalem took little note of the 120 followers of the Nazarene gathered for ten days. But when the disciples were deeply moved upon by God, 'the multitude came together'. And they were 'confounded', 'amazed', 'perplexed' and they finally just

gave up trying to discover a rationale for the pheno-
menon and asked, 'What does this mean?' It was then
—and not until then—that Peter could stand up and
say, 'This is that . . . !' and thus present Christ. Now this
is always ideally the context of great evangelism. The
outside world becomes so perplexed by the wonder of
what God has done and is doing for His Church that
they begin asking questions. It is in this kind of setting
that the gospel can truly be communicated. Surely, all
of us earnestly pray for such a move of God's Spirit
upon His Church.

Finally, on the day of Pentecost, Christ was preached.
The disciples had but one message. This does not mean
that later we do not see the New Testament Church
ministering in many different ways. They were not
afraid of the social implications of the gospel, for example. It surely does not mean they did not confront
men in their own life situation and thus approach them
with that particular aspect of the good news that was
most appealing and relevant. But whether we see
Stephen addressing the biblical-oriented Sanhedrin, Peter
appealing to the God-fearing Gentile Cornelius, or Paul
preaching to the philosophical sophisticates of Athens,
they approached these different people and with their
different references of thought by simply presenting
Christ as the answer to life's basic needs. Here is an inescapable principle for effective evangelistic endeavour
and a vital part of a sound theology of mission.

Now it is recognised, as we bring this chapter to a
close, that this mere skeleton of a theology of evangelism needs much meat hung on the bare bones.[16] But if
the Spirit can breathe upon us, it is hoped that these
bones can live. With this framework of theology, therefore, let us move on to consider the more practical
aspects and problems of evangelism.

1. C. E. Autrey, *Basic Evangelism*, p. 13.

2. A. Skevington Wood, *Evangelism, Its Theology and Practice* (Grand Rapids, Zondervan, 1966), p. 11.

3. C. E. Autrey, op. cit., p. 16.

4. Culbert G. Rutenber, *The Reconciling Gospel* (Philadelphia, Judson Press, 1960), p. 41.

5. ibid., p. 41.

6. ibid., p. 46.

7. Michael Green, *Evangelism in the Early Church* (London, Hodder and Stoughton, 1970), pp. 53–4.

8. Leon Morris, *The Apostolic Preaching of the Cross* (London, Tyndale Press, 1955), p. 12.

9. ibid., p. 54.

10. ibid., p. 279.

11. Culbert G. Rutenberer, op. cit., p. 48.

12. ibid., p. 55.

13. The volume entitled *Agape and Eros* by Andres Nygren is a classic on this theme.

14. *The Church for Others*, p. 75.

15. R. H. C. Lenski, *The Interpretation of the Acts of the Apostles* (Minneapolis, Augsburg Publishing House, 1934), p. 355.

16. In the closing section of this book is found a bibliography of helpful works on evangelism in addition to the references cited in the notes.

3

A Strategy of Outreach
for Today

We have attempted to present the obligations of the
pastor relative to developing an evangelistic Church.
But most pastors are no doubt quite knowledgeable of
their responsibility to mission. Few have failed to grasp
the implications of the Great Commission concerning
their ministry. Further, one would suppose that a large
percentage have developed something of a theology of
evangelism and are to a greater or lesser degree thus
motivated to engage in the grand enterprise. The question that constantly comes up, however, as I address
ministerial groups and church leadership conferences is,
how can we evangelise today? There seems to be almost
a spirit of frustration as evangelistically-minded Christians seek ways and means of implementing into
practical service their theology of mission. This is understandable, especially in western Europe and America.
We have never lived in a psychological and sociological
atmosphere comparable to today's revolutionary spirit.
The old forms to which many congregations are shackled
just do not suffice to communicate the good news to
contemporary man. What can be done? Is there an
effective strategy for outreach that will work today?
I believe we can answer this query quite affirmatively.
And the solution is to be found in a principle as old as
the Scriptures themselves. The key to effective mission in
this or any generation rests essentially in the New Testament concept of the service of the laity.

The New Testament principle of the lay-centred ministry

May I be bold and state quite categorically at the very outset that unless the Church recaptures and implements the principle of a lay-centred ministry, I see little hope of fulfilling the commission to evangelise our day. And this, of course, leads one to conclude that there is little hope for any resurgence of dynamic growth in the local churches until the principle is incorporated. This we have already emphasised, but may we now examine the concept in some detail.

It hardly seems necessary to present any kind of apologetic for the principle of a lay-centred ministry. Most pastors would be only too happy to see their lay people go to work. Moreover, most are aware, as Green tells us, that 'Christianity was from its inception a lay movement, and so it continued for a remarkably long time.'[1] Ministry for the early Christians was a happy, unselfconscious effort. They just went about quite naturally sharing their faith, 'gossiping the gospel', as it were. They were zealous, enthusiastic; they could not help but speak of the things they had experienced. They were not 'professionals'; they were unpaid. As a consequence, they were taken seriously—especially was this true among the lower classes—and the movement spread like wildfire. As Green points out :

> All of this makes it abundantly clear that in contrast to the present day, when Christianity is highly intellectualised and dispensed by a professional clergy to a constituency increasingly confined to the middle classes, in the early days the faith was spontaneously spread by informal evangelists, and had its greatest appeal among the working classes.[2]

Simply put, through the ministry of these first-century laymen the masses were effectually reached with the gospel.

Now it is reasonably conclusive, in the light of what has been said above, that in the Early Church there was little if any distinction between full-time ministers and the laity, at least in the sense of responsibility to spread the good news. Every Christian was an evangelist. They well understood, as Goyder, a layman himself, has graphically put it, there are to be 'no passengers in the church. All are called'.[3]

It is regrettable that in these early years of the Church clericalism soon began to develop. More and more the clergy assumed command of the evangelistic mission and the layman was slowly squeezed out. Thus the clergy began to dominate the laity in a very unscriptural fashion. Through the centuries this attitude hardened until in the course of time the English word 'lay' has become a synonym for 'amateur' as over against 'professional', or 'unqualified' as opposed to 'expert'. How often we hear today, 'I'm just a layman'. This can usually be taken as an apology for not being able to do something very well. Of course, it is true that some church members have not objected too vigorously to this development. More than a few have acquired a sort of 'spectator mentality' concerning their church, and what they seem to want, as Sir John Lawrence states, is 'a building which looks like a church; a clergyman dressed in a way he approves; services of the kind he's been used to, *and to be left alone*.'[4] Such laymen have little if any real interest in evangelism, let alone actively engaging in the task.

On the other hand, however, there have been reactions to the clericalism of the contemporary Church. Some have reacted very strongly, hence we have movements like the Quakers and Plymouth Brethren who have virtually rejected the idea of a professional clergy. Other reactions have not been quite as cavalier, but have nevertheless been very real. In the more traditional churches, for example, some laymen, along with several ministers, are asking if in today's world the clergy are necessary.

One would suppose, however, that the bulk of Christians just accept some sort of dualism and acknowledge the need of ministers and laymen alike, but have no real concept of the respective roles they play in the mission activity of the Church. Yet a dualism of this sort is never truly satisfying and is a constant source of inefficiency if not irritation. Can such a situation find a resolution? It seems that it can in the biblical concept of

The Church as the body of Christ
There are many figures used in the New Testament to describe the people of God, the Church. There are the concepts of the Church as the bride of Christ, God's vineyard, God's flock, the Kingdom, the Father's family, God's building, a holy priesthood, the new Israel, a holy nation, and so on. But one of the most graphic, and that which seemed to be a favourite of Paul's, is to view the Church as a body. This idea has two important implications relative to our consideration. First, as a body has different parts with different functions, so the Church. To say all members in a church are just the same is rather ridiculous, for they obviously are not. Abilities and gifts vary with each member. Thus to contend that all members are to do the same thing in mission activity is untenable. 'Are all apostles? Are all prophets? Are all teachers? Do all work miracles? Do all possess gifts of healing? Do all speak in tongues? Do all interpret? For as the body is one and has many members, and all the members of the body though many, are one body, so it is with Christ. For by one Spirit we were all baptised into one body.' (1 Cor. 12:29–30; 12–13). There is a diversity of members and corresponding functions in the local church that must be recognised.

But secondly, and here we get more to the point, the metaphor of the body strongly suggests that in the Church's diversity there is a central, inescapable unity. All the members stand equal and one *before God*. It is the one and same Spirit that enables all Christians to say, 'Jesus is Lord'. Moreover, as the body is a whole, so also is its basic task. The commission to evangelise is given to the entire body. John Stott reminds us that 'the essential unity of the Church, originating in the call of God and illustrated in the metaphors of Scripture, leads us to this conclusion: the responsibilities which God has entrusted to His Church He has entrusted to His *whole* Church.'[5] Now it is just here that clericalism, anti-clericalism and an unsatisfying dualism can be resolved. A clear grasp of this unity in diversity of the body metaphor can save us from all three errors. It is the Church as a diversified yet unified body that fulfils its purpose in worship and ministry.

What relationship then is implied between the so-called laity and clergy in the body metaphor? First, we must eradicate the error of interpreting the laity from the standpoint of the clergy; for example, the clergy does, the laity does not, etc. Rather, we must define the clergy in relation to the body,[6] i.e. the laity are the whole people of God and the clergy are given the privilege of over-sight, shepherding, equipping them for service. This we discussed in Chapter 1. Several figures may be helpful here to show the proper relationship. Elton Trueblood, for example, likens the clergyman to the coach of a football team. The coach instructs, teaches, motivates and helps direct the play, but the team (the laity) has the major role in actually playing the game. Or perhaps we can see the minister as a filling station attendant. The layman gets his car filled up with fuel and kept in repair by the man at the station. But the layman does the actual running of the car, not the attendant or mechanics. Of course, the minister is a Christian too! And by virtue of that fact he must also 'play the game' and 'drive the car'. But this is essentially because he is a Christian, not simply because he is a clergyman. In other words, he is the helper and equipper of the layman so that the lay-man can get on with the job, not vice versa as is so often the case. As Stott has told us, '. . . if anybody belongs to anybody in the Church, it is not the laity who belongs to the clergy, but the clergy who belongs to the laity.'[7] With this relationship in the diversified but integrated body, the work can effectively go forward. It is to this end and principle we need give our earnest attention.

Now if such is the relationship in the body, a significant responsibility in the pastoral equipping of the laity for mission is eminently implied.

The place of Christian education in outreach
It is quite evident that if the foregoing principles are taken seriously and implemented, something of a revolution will take place in most congregations. To move the layman out of his comfortable pew and into the arena of evangelism is no mean undertaking. It will first of all take motivation. Years of relative inactivity concerning mission on the part of the average church member will not be changed easily. And again, it would seem that the basic responsibility, under God, to motivate these Christians, is the pastor's charge.

But let us assume there are a number of members in the local church who are willing to undertake active service in the call to evangelise. The next demanding task is then to begin the educational process that will equip God's people for their ministry. The Lambeth Conference in 1968 made the following appeal: 'No one wants untrained troops . . . We need a Christian education explosion comparable to that in the secular world.' Then it was resolved: 'The Conference believes that there is an urgent need for increase in the quantity and quality of training available for lay people for their task in the world.'[8] Thus it is apt for one to conclude that Christian education is perhaps one of the most single pressing needs in our churches today if we are to begin effectively evangelising.

The nature of an adequate Christian education programme

As a Christian education programme is undertaken, it must be recognised that there are several elements that are ingredient to an adequate educational structure in a local church. First, a valid and comprehensive *objective* of Christian education is essential.[9] Roger L. Shinn gives the three objects of Christian education, based on Mark 12:29–31 (where Jesus commands one to love God and his fellows): (1) to grow in relation to God; (2) to develop trustful and responsible relations with others; and (3) to become a whole person.[10] Quite obviously, without some such basic principles as a goal and basis for education, few Christians will ever become equipped to engage successfully in mission.

Secondly, the *content* of Christian education must be as comprehensive as God's redemptive purpose for man. Revealed truth forms the foundation of the curriculum. And such truths must present the spiritual experience of Christ in its real life setting. It reveals and interprets God's self-disclosure in human history. It sets forth the meaning and demands of discipleship today. Above all, it presents God as redeeming contemporary man in His Son, through the agency of the Church.

Thirdly, as implied above, an adequate Christian education programme must grow out of the needs of man where he is in today's world. The great temptation in Christian education is to become too much 'content-centred' as over against 'person-centred', i.e. to be so concerned about *what* we teach that we almost ignore *who* we teach and *why*. After all, it is people that matter so much to God.

Fourthly, the *function* of Christian education should help persons fulfil God's intention for them. Of course, this is implied in the entire concept of Christian teaching. This idea will be expanded as we discuss the actual nature of accomplishing one's ministry in the life of outreach.

Finally, Christian education must be seen more broadly than just equipping the Church for its task—central and vital as that is. It must be broad enough to reach out into the unbelieving community also and confront people with God's revealed truth. Jesus the teacher is an obvious example of this principle. A. Leonard Griffith has well said, '. . . He *challenges* us, this man outside the Church. . . . He challenges us to reach Him and commend our faith to Him. He challenges us simply because He is there, just as Mount Everest challenged adventurous men until they finally conquered it.'[11] And, to carry the simile on, if the local church made the preparation and effort in its Christian education programme of outreach in as dedicated a fashion as Sir Edmund Hillary and his party did in their attempt to conquer Mount Everest, the results would be similar.

Now such a comprehensive Christian education programme calls for mature and imaginative leadership; a leadership that may exist only in the pastor and a few members at the moment. It is very evident that in many congregations leaders will have to be trained before the real task of educating the bulk of the laity can even begin. This is so often painfully true. But this must not deter one from beginning. A start must be made. What then are the qualities we must look for and attempt to create in those who shall lead? A pastor, the Rev. R. Rodney Collins of London, has set forth what is to be sought and developed in leaders:

Qualifications for Leadership

1. A humble dependence on God whose Holy Spirit guides into all the truth (John 16:13). A young married couple leading an international Bible study group in a London church confessed, 'If we try to do it in our own strength we get flustered and

74

frustrated. We have learned to trust the Lord to help us.'

2. A readiness to stir up (2 Tim. 1:6) and not neglect (1 Tim. 4:14) one's gifts.

3. An appreciation of the place of comprehensive Christian education in the Church's life, in accordance with the great commission, 'Make disciples . . . teaching them . . .' (the present participle implying a continuous process, not only preparing believers for baptism but continuing afterwards with a view to practical Christian living).

4. Teachability, especially in regard to modern educational techniques and methods. 'Give instruction to a wise man and he will be still wiser . . .' (Prov. 9:9). 'You then who teach others, will you not teach yourself?' (Rom. 2:21).

5. Faithfulness, rather than exceptional ability. 'Faithful men . . . will be able to teach others also' (2 Tim. 2:2).

6. A love of people and a real concern for them, rather than a passion for talking to them!

7. A respect for others which enables one to accept criticism and profit by it (Rom. 12:3).

8. Sensitivity in personal relationships. The good and efficient work of a dedicated leader can be vitiated if his relations with others lack a sensitive awareness of their feelings, needs and desires.

9. The ability to deal with personality problems especially those arising out of the voluntary nature of Christian service.

10. An optimistic spirit inspired by Christian hope which will not easily be depressed by difficulties, disappointments and discouragements.[12]

These qualifications may seem a rather large order and I suppose it is never completely attained by any. Yet it is a worthy goal and goals give direction when taken seriously.

Let us now pause for just a moment and summarise what we have been calling for to this point. We are asking that the whole Church get involved in mission on the basis that the entire body has received the commission to evangelise. In this light, the laity must be equipped for the task. Hence we have stressed the importance and nature of Christian education. But before the mass of church members can be taught, leadership—mature leadership—must be developed in order that they may adequately teach others. And the overriding implication is that the pastor is the one who must most probably 'get the ball rolling'. Now if such is to be the immediate goal, it is essential to recognise the necessity of the pastor giving himself, at least to some extent, to what is commonly called church administration and programming.

The place of church administration and organisation in mission

Administration, it would appear, is a bad word for some pastors. 'Is it not outside the minister's spiritual call?' pastors often ask. Now it is easy to be a bit super-pious on this point and hold that ministers are to give themselves only to the 'spiritual' aspects of ministry. The deacons or stewards or lay leaders can handle the mundane things like administration, it is often thought. But is such an attitude justifiable? I seriously doubt it. In the first place, it should help us if we can come to realise just what church administration is. Lindgren defines it in these words :

> Purposeful church administration is the involvement of the church in the discovery of her nature and mission and in moving in a coherent and comprehensive manner toward providing such experience as will enable the church to utilise all her resources and personnel in the fulfilment of her mission of making known God's love for all men.[13]

Now that hardly sounds 'unspiritual'! Surely a pastor can see his responsibilities there. Even a secular definition of administration has significant implications for a church when its principles are translated into the life of a Christian congregation. For example, Ordway Tead tells us:

> Administration is the process and agency which is responsible for the determination of the aims for which an organisation and its management are to strive, which establishes the broad policies under which they are to operate, and which gives general oversight to the continuing effectiveness of the total operation in reaching the objectives sought.[14]

If one understands the nature and objectives of mission, even this is not 'unspiritual' for God's ministers. Dr W. L. Howse has well stated:

> For years many leaders have felt that administration was fine for the business world but that it was too secular for churches. The recognition of administration as a church process will remove the stigma of secularism and make administration a useful tool for churches. Good administration is nothing more than following correct processes in getting essential work done well.[15]

Having been a pastor myself for many years, I finally came to the conclusion—somewhat reluctantly I must admit—that serious church administration is a responsibility of the pastor. It is a responsibility he cannot avoid. Moreover it is one he should not want to escape. Actually, to a greater or lesser degree, he does it anyway. Therefore, he should do it well. It does not seem 'spiritual' at all to me to engage in this or any part of the ministry in a half-hearted, negligent manner. If God has entrusted to a pastor a leadership role in the church, administration is vital and inescapable. Therefore, for the sake of the Kingdom, he should do it well—very well and with zest. It is just a part of the ministry in today's kind of world. Of course, I am not calling on pastors to become sanctified 'wheeler-dealers'. But let's face reality; in our contemporary, technologically-oriented society, and in the face of the vital needs of developing a dynamic educational programme in the local church, I do not see how the spiritually-minded pastor can side-step his responsibilities in the area of church administration and programming.

In the light, then, of the need and call for good church administration, George Wilson has set out three important principles:

1. Administration exists to accomplish something —in this case, the work of the church or work which the church designates. The main question which the church must face in this regard is not whether or not it will have administration. The question the church faces in this regard is a choice of good versus bad administration. Any attempt to get anything done through the efforts of others *is* administration of some kind. The question is, what kind?

2. Objectives and commensurate goals are indispensable to good administration. Timeless intention to act, coupled with specific actions planned in such a light help the church to shape being out of co-operative chaos, i.e. mutually created by competing organisations.

3. People are central. A writer has stated, 'Leadership is measured by the led.' There is no progress if people do not make progress. Study of the biblical documents is not planned as an exercise for computers or machines, but for persons. Training to minister in Christ's name—to go 'to him outside

the camp, bearing the stigma he bore' (Heb. 13:14, N.E.B.), is not a task designed to be accomplished by empty classrooms or sanctuaries, but by people committed to ministering in the world.[16]

Thus the minister begins the task of 'equipping the saints for the work of the ministry' (Eph. 4:12). But what are the structures of ministry that are to be created? To this important issue we must now address ourselves.

The 'gifts of the Spirit' as the pattern in organisation for ministry

Perhaps the reason church administration has often seemed just a little tedious to us is because of the problems of finding a really satisfying way to organise the local church into effective ministry. It so often appears that one is just organising for organisation's sake and taking quite a humanistic approach in so doing. There is little satisfaction in organising a church simply to keep the machine ticking over. We may even feel at times that our church programming is a mere manipulating of people. The results thus seem to be that we are forever putting square pegs in round holes and no one is genuinely satisfied and the work suffers. I am convinced, however, there is a pattern that can be employed that has its roots deeply implanted in the Scriptures and in the dynamic of the Holy Spirit's working among His people. And if such be the case, satisfaction and success can be expected. I refer to the biblical principle which Paul in particular laboured to implement in the churches he founded, namely that of Christians serving in the context of the 'gifts of the Spirit'—the *charismata*.

I must be frank and confess that in approaching such a theme, it is done with some hesitation. First, I fear misunderstanding by some. The biblical concept of gifts is often grossly misinterpreted—especially is this so today. Perversions of the teaching have left few churches untouched. Secondly, there is always the danger of being 'labelled'. And labels are usually quite emotive—to the extent that at times some may even be tempted to throw out the baby with the bath water. But I trust neither of these apprehensions will be evoked by what I wish to say on this most important issue. Perhaps the single most important fact to realise as we take up this theme is that these gifts of the Spirit are given to the Church for ministry. They are not for individual, spiritual indulgence of any kind. The Holy Spirit imparts them essentially so that believers may be more effective in their service for Christ. If we keep this principle before us we can keep ourselves from many errors.

Now clearly, here is a teaching that is little discussed in the contemporary Church—at least in a positive, constructive manner. Yet it had significant prominence in the life of ministry in the Early Church. Three rather lengthy passages are devoted to the theme in Paul's writings: Eph. 4:4–16, 1 Cor. 12–14, Rom. 12:3–8. A number of things need to be said concerning the concept.

The New Testament declares that when Christ ascended back to the Father, He 'led a host of captives and He gave gifts to men' (Eph. 4:8). These gifts are the consequence of the presence of the 'Spirit of promise' who indwells all believers. As previously stated, they are given by our Lord for the purpose of equipping His people for the work of the ministry. It is important to distinguish these gifts of the Spirit from the fruits of the Spirit (Gal. 5:22–4). The fruits are the manifestation of the Spirit in the daily life of the Christian to make him Christlike in character. The gifts are the manifestation of the Spirit through the believer to make his service effectual.

In the three primary New Testament passages mentioned above, the spiritual gifts are enumerated. First, in 1 Corinthians 12:28–30 we read the following list:

1. Apostles
2. Prophets
3. Teachers
4. Workers of miracles
5. The healing of sick
6. Serviceable ministries (helps)
7. Government (oversight)
8. Varieties of tongues

Secondly, Romans 12:3–8 presents some additions to the above list in the following:

1. Prophecy
2. Ministrations
3. Teacher
4. Exhortation
5. Giver
6. Ruler
7. He who shows mercy

Finally, we read in 1 Corinthians 12:8–10:

1. Utterance of wisdom
2. Utterance of knowledge
3. Faith
4. Healing
5. Miracles
6. Prophecy
7. Discernment of spirits
8. Varieties of tongues
9. Interpretations of tongues

It is quite evident from the above that the principle of the gifts of the Spirit have singular importance for the entire work of the ministry. Therefore, they cannot be taken lightly by the Church. Paul says, 'It is important, brethren, that you should have clear knowledge on the subject of spiritual gifts' (I Cor. 12 : 1, Weymouth). Now what can be said about these gifts? Initially, it is clear that some gifts are obviously the Christians themselves with particular ministries, e.g. apostles, prophets, teachers, etc. In other cases the emphasis is upon the gift itself rather than the individual who is gifted, e.g. faith, varieties of tongues, etc. Yet this distinction should not be pressed too far. Perhaps the simplest thing to say is that a gift apart from a believer to exercise the gift is meaningless and a believer who is not gifted is a relatively ineffectual Christian servant. The gift and the gifted form the warp and woof of the theme.

Secondly, the gifts of the Spirit are not to be confused with natural talents. Though all have natural abilities —abilities that God will surely use in his service—the spiritual gifts are not these *per se*. *The Expositor's Bible* points this out by stating, 'They [the believers] were endowed at their conversion . . . with certain powers *which they had not previously possessed*, and which were due to the influence of the Holy Spirit.'[17]

Then, the gifts must be seen as spiritual powers that the believer must exercise only under the control of the Holy Spirit. They are not to be used simply when and how the believer wishes, let alone to enjoy selfishly. As the writer in the *International Critical Commentary* declares, 'The operator . . . is always God : every one of the gifts in every person that manifests them . . . is bestowed and set in motion by Him.'[18] It is quite obvious that Paul wrote the lengthy passage found in I Corinthians 12–14 to direct the use of the gifts and to save the Church from just such abuses.

To summarise, the gifts must be understood as a grace-gift, a supernatural endowment, a spiritual manifestation of God the Spirit through the believer for the enrichment of the Body, for the development and work of the ministry. As has been said, 'It is simply the Holy Spirit working through us in a given manner, at the time He, the Spirit, chooses, for the carrying out of the

ministry to which we have been appointed of God.'[19]
The American Commentary states, 'They are all, however various, to be employed in the service of Him, the
one Lord.'[20] Moreover, it must be emphasised that the
Holy Spirit distributes gifts to every believer. Paul seems
to state that there are no exceptions, *every* believer has
a gift or gifts apportioned to him. Lenski declares that
the emphasis rests primarily on the dative in 1 Corinthians 12:7, thus implying that 'to each one . . . each
believer has his gifts, and every bestowal of a gift is for
the common good'.[21]

Now at this point it appears important that we gain
something of a grasp of the actual meaning of the various gifts and the purpose for which each is intended.
Perhaps the following general classification will help:

1. For the proclamation of God's self-disclosure;
the gift of prophecy or preaching.
2. For teaching the divine revelation; the gift of
teaching.
3. For enabling God's blessing to flow into needy
lives; the gift of faith that enables believers to rest
upon God's promises and trust in the power that is
beyond the sphere of human possibilities.
4. For the revelation of God's will and purpose in
matters; the gift of wisdom so that God's purpose
in His word can be grasped.
5. For understanding the practical application of
eternal principles in daily experience; the utterance
of knowledge.
6. For protection against evil; the gift of discernment of spirits.
7. For the practical manifestation of the love of
Christ there are three gifts: mercy, the Paraclete
gift and giving.
8. For maintaining order in the life and work of
the Church; the gift of government. This is surely
not far from what we have been speaking about

when we discussed the importance of church administration.

9. For help in the community; the gift of serviceable ministries or 'helps'.

10. As special signs of God's power and presence, there are four gifts: miracles, healings, tongues and interpretations of tongues.[22]

A few things must be said concerning this brief outline of the gifts. In the first place, it is obvious that the number of gifts found in the Scriptures is comparatively small. This leads to the conclusion that each gift listed must be understood as a designation of a *class* of gifts. In each classification there will quite naturally be many variations. Circumstances, situations and needs vary from culture to culture and from generation to generation. Thus the biblical gifts must be seen as flexible in their manifestations so as to meet the relevant needs of all people at all times.

Secondly, a study of all the gifts of the Spirit make it evident that God has provided in full measure for all needs of the Church in its growth, worship and ministry. The organisation of the local church, its government, its instruction and equipping, its worship, its ministry of witness and its entire corporate life are fully cared for. As John Short in *The Interpreter's Bible* has said: 'Let there be among the Corinthian Christians, and in every Christian church in any age, clear recognition of the simple truth that in such a divinely appointed organism as the body of Christ, for its vitality and its effective witness, a variety of functions is required.'[23] And the Spirit will surely see to it that no part of work suffers for lack of a gift if the church is open to His lead.

Thirdly, the principle of spiritual gifts is what truly makes the local church a body. The writer in *The Expositor's Greek Testament* points out that the *charismata* of the Spirit are 'portioned out amongst the members of

Christ, for manifold and reciprocal service to *His body*'.[24] Paul sets the whole theme in this important context. The Holy Spirit bestows these gifts 'as He wills' (1 Cor. 12 : 11). And surely He will not create a body that is all hands or eyes or feet. He will develop a perfectly functioning and unified body. I am quite sure that a church never becomes a unified whole by mere organisation alone. It is the Spirit that creates the body. Barclay states in commenting on the Corinthian church, 'The whole idea of Paul . . . is to stress the essential unity of the church.'[25]

Finally, it is when church members employ their gifts under the direction of the Holy Spirit that the church is built up and strengthened and the work progresses and thus the *missio Dei* is carried on. As Lenski has said, '. . . each member of the church benefits the entire body by rightly employing his particular gift'.[26] The work is God's mission and it is quite clear in the New Testament that the work is energised by the Spirit through the gifted church, local and catholic.

We cannot undertake here a detailed exegesis of the important passages on spiritual gifts although such a study would be tremendously helpful. But perhaps it has now been made clear by this short discussion on the theme that, as Barclay says, when a church functions on the basis of the gifts of the Spirit, 'The picture we get is the picture of a Church vividly alive. Things happened; in fact astonishing things happened. Life was heightened and intensified and sensitised. There was nothing flat and dull and ordinary about the . . . Church.'[27] And this is what we all desire today for the body, and what we must see if we are to evangelise our contemporary generation.

In the light of all that has been said concerning spiritual gifts, here is the suggestion I wish to put forward : the church should be geared in its organisational life so that the members of the church can exercise the gifts that have been committed to them by the Holy Spirit.

Now it may well be that this is already being done to a greater or lesser degree implicitly. But what is being called for is an *explicit* structuring of the organisational pattern of the local church along these lines. In other words, the church's programme should be developed in such a manner that the Holy Spirit can manifest Himself in and through His people as He wills. This obviously calls for a number of revolutionary approaches.

Initially, therefore, we must move towards placing far more confidence in our gifted church members. As an Anglican layman has expressed it:

> Why is it the Church today will not trust its members? Why does the Church so often decline to recognise and to accept the activity of the Spirit among unregulated groups of Christians? Why is all initiative in the Church expected and presumed to derive from the clergy? It is because we have substituted for the biblical doctrine of the Holy Spirit as ruler in the Church, a doctrine of our own, unknown to Scripture, the authority of professionalism. In regard to the conducting of services and the administration of the sacraments the authority of the ministry is not in question. But we are now considering the training and commissioning of Christian men and women to take lay initiative in the world...[28]

If we take seriously the lay-centred ministry concept and genuinely believe that God's Spirit empowers and gives gifts to all Christians, we must trust these believers to get on with the job. After all, is not this what we mean by the priesthood of all believers? And it is more than merely incidental that such an approach saves the layman from feeling so inadequate for the task and responsibility that is clearly his.

Further, as already stressed, there will probably be quite a change in the present structures of the local

86

church programme. I do not mean a little change here and there or merely using more pop tunes in the services or the preacher using 'groovy' talk when he preaches. I am suggesting a real revolution that organises a church on the basis of what spiritual gifts are manifest in the corporate life of the body rather than just trying to prop up old, irrelevant, inept structures. In the concluding section of this chapter some guidelines on how to implement this principle will be considered.

Moreover, as we have discussed earlier, much instruction, Christian teaching and help must be given to implement the principle. Most Christians are grossly ignorant concerning the work of the Holy Spirit. I should suppose the bulk of God's people do not even know Christians are gifted by the Holy Spirit, let alone know what gifts the Spirit would manifest through them. A real process of education on pneumatology is usually needed as the gifts will need sharpening and developing. Also, it may well be that many misconceptions concerning the work of the Holy Spirit will have to be eradicated. Further, as previously pointed out, may I stress again that the minister must be on guard to protect his people from being swept away in some movement that reports itself to be of the Holy Spirit, but though it may speak much of particular gifts of the Spirit, bears little fruit of the Spirit. It is all too clear that not a few Christians have fallen victim to gross errors concerning the *charismata* of the Spirit. Paul was on guard for the believers in Corinth: so also must be the contemporary pastor.

Finally, the minister will have to give himself to the development and administration of these new goals. Changing basic approaches and structures will be difficult. But these changes seem mandatory, and although the pastor may be somewhat reluctant to give himself to the increased administrative responsibilities of developing new programmes, I see no other way out.

But there it is! The *missio Dei* committed to the whole body; and the layman, recognising that he is gifted by the Spirit, thus desires to engage in ministry. He now needs church structures through which he can serve in relation to his specific gifts. He desperately needs development through Christian education. And the pastor stands as the layman's servant to see that he gets it all. Thus the church becomes a truly unified, functioning body being built up in the faith, and the *missio Dei* goes forward. Sounds great! But can it work?

Some practical suggestions

At the outset, let me say that I believe what we find in the Scriptures by way of principle can always be implemented in a pragmatic way in the local church. If God has called all of His people into mission, then I believe the bulk of God's people can be led to perform the task. What I wish to present in this closing section of the chapter, therefore, are some practical suggestions on how to get started in church-centred evangelistic activity. Here is something I should hope that can be commenced immediately. It calls for honesty and bravery, but a beginning must be undertaken. This most pastors deeply feel, and as a friend of mine once said, 'The world will not be won by people who stand around wringing their hands.' We have bewailed the condition of the Church long enough. We have diagnosed our ills until one feels almost like a spiritual hypochondriac. The call is now for action, even if it is only a beginning. Now granted the suggestions I wish to make may be a mere beginning, but they have been undertaken by others and God has honoured the honest effort. At least it is a start.

First, therefore, from the standpoint of the corporate service of the church, let us be willing to face the fact that probably many of the present structures of church life will need some changing. We have discussed this almost *ad nauseum*. But how can it actually be done? That is the crunch. We all know only too well that there is always resistance—often strong resistance—to change. May I therefore suggest initially that the pastor who is keenly aware of the needs, gather around himself a group of spiritual church leaders. It would be best in most instances to have a representative group from the life of the church, i.e. the directors of the various departmental aspects of the church programme, if at all possible. But above all, let them be the ones who are spiritually oriented and open to the purposes of God in mission. I think it vital to choose no one but spiritually-minded people even if only one or two are available. I do not intend to imply we are to be judges of how well our church members are related to God. But one can usually discern those who are open to the moving of the Holy Spirit. Then the pastor should begin with this group; teaching, encouraging, challenging and informing them concerning the need of evangelism and the openness that is required if the church is going to be effectively geared for outreach. They should be made to become vividly aware of what the goals and mission of the church actually are. It is essential and foundational, it seems to me, to know where we want to go. So often the church keeps merely ticking over because it has no real goals before it. As has been said, if you have no goal, you will hit it every time. But after much prayer, education and heart-searching, and when the pastor feels his group is genuinely committed to mission and even zealous for it, they should sit down together, with their goals before them, and scrutinise the entire present church programme. Let them examine and evaluate each and every facet of the structured life of the church. Let them be honest about each phase, asking these questions: Does it line up with the goals of the church? Does it really have relevance for today's world? Does it honestly meet needs? Does it genuinely further the Kingdom of God through the life of the church? Does it accord with scriptural principles such as the exercising of spiritual gifts, etc.? These are not easy questions to ask. It calls for objectivity, integrity, and not a little courage. We all have vested interests in our present church programme

and to be objective and honest is often painful.
But I see it as essential that we analyse what we *are*
doing in the light of what we, under God, *should* be
doing. In the appendix of this book a guide for conducting such a survey is given. Many churches have
followed just such an approach and have often found
it very helpful.

Now if the answers to the above questions can be
given in such a way that we can unqualifiedly say that
a certain part of the church programme lines up with
scriptural goals and principles, then it is ridiculous to
change that phase of the programme, let alone throw it
out. Change for change's sake alone is unworthy. But if
it becomes clear, as it often does, that certain programmes are archaic, outmoded, irrelevant and not
meeting genuine needs—thus superfluous to mission—
then let us be honest and courageous enough to change
them. In other words, if it is dead, give it a decent
burial.

Now granted, this is negative and rather destructive.
There is, however, a positive side to the coin. There is a
constructive work to be done. After a careful diagnosis
of the present structures and the tentative (I emphasise
tentative) elimination of the irrelevant, then there must
begin the rebuilding of a positive, relevant and dynamic
new church programme. Two vital principles must be
kept in mind in this endeavour; first, the church's goals
must be clearly before the group, and, secondly, the new
structures must be built on the principle of involving
the laity in the programme, thus allowing them to exercise their gifts. And we must remember that our structures are to be geared in such a fashion that we are
preparing for our mission in the world. In other words,
as has been often said, we must give attention to 'go
structures' far more than 'come structures', at least as
far as evangelistic outreach is concerned. This will obviously take much prayer, thought and time. It will
be demanding for the pastor and the mission action

group as well. Moreover, I think it wise in most situations for all this negative and positive work on the church programme to be done in closed committee, at least in the earlier stages. Often the whole church, at the outset, is just not ready for such changes. But after a tentative new church programme is developed by this mission group, the real task of educating the church must be undertaken. Of course, the educational process will be going on all during this initial spade work. What is vital to recognise is that the church must be informed and inspired concerning mission and what is needed to fulfil the commission. Here patience, perseverance, understanding and love must be the key-note. Christians move slowly—some will not move at all. But with the leadership and power of the Holy Spirit the church can be challenged, educated and inspired to follow the Spirit's lead into a new church structure geared for mission outreach.

It cannot be emphasised too strongly that the educational process must be patiently followed. It is bound to take time. Perhaps months and even years will be necessary in some churches. But it must be done for the sake of mission. Of course, there will be those in the church who will not buy it at any cost. What do we do then? Well, in love, and I underline *in love*, they must be bypassed and the work go on. Mission is vital and if there are those who stand in the way they must be understood and loved, but dealt with as our Lord Himself did.

Now it is true that such an approach to church programming demands insight into community needs. I would suggest, therefore, that a careful survey of the community as well as of the church itself be undertaken by the action group. Issues such as the special sociological aspects of the community to which the church hopes to minister must be grasped and understood. The group should come alive to the specific needs of their particular community. The geographical area and its influences on church life should be considered. We need to know the general characteristics of those whom we are attempting to reach, i.e. what is their social, educational, financial, status or level, and so on. As the report of the Evangelical Alliance, *On the Other Side* has pointed out, we must become far more conscious of the sociological aspects of mission.

Furthermore, the tentative programme that is to be implemented must be kept flexible. Some new programmes attempted may prove quite unsuccessful when they are actually executed. If such be the case, let us be brave once again and change them and try something else. The mistake of getting wedded to the new programme can be as deadly as being wedded to the old. It must be remembered it is not a sin to fail, the sin lies in never attempting anything lest one should fail. The local church must be subject to constant change in its programming for mission if it is to improve its methodologies and keep abreast of the ever-changing community.

Of course, we have obviously been discussing that which relates essentially to the structured, corporate life of the church. There is much that the members can do, and should be led to do, on an individual basis. We shall discuss this aspect of mission in a moment. What is vital at this point is to see that here is a start for the pastor-evangelist to begin gearing his church for mission. True, he may have to begin with very few interested leaders. But here is something he can do. This is something that can be begun now. As already mentioned, it has been undertaken in many congregations and done quite successfully.

This chapter is probably already too long, so we cannot go into a lengthy discussion of some of the new areas where structured outreach has proved effective today. Suffice it, therefore, simply to mention some of these areas of outreach and present a few case studies to illustrate how effective some of them are.

First, the principle of group dynamics should be

investigated. The upsurge of interest in small groups, e.g. house groups, Bible study groups, young people's groups, all-age Sunday school, retreats, etc. has proved most useful. The church that overlooks this field of mission endeavour and church edification is ignoring a vast reservoir of productive blessing. A few examples of success in these fields of outreach may prove helpful.

As most of us know, one of the most exciting new methods of outreach is the house group. Of course, it is not new as a principle. It can be traced right back to the New Testament. But a new impetus has been given to it lately. Many churches have implemented the idea into very fruitful endeavours. For example, the Rev. Paul Tucker of the East London Tabernacle—a very difficult inner-city area—has had unusual success with the methodology. There are several lay people in this church who have a regular programme of house meetings. The leaders keep their homes open at all times (this seems important), but once a week they have a structured group meeting. A regular, solid attendance has been built up. They have learned to be very flexible and not to be shocked or put off by what they experience from those who attend. Moreover, they have learned to communicate to their attenders, and to the entire community for that matter, that they truly care. Thus they have little difficulty in attracting the pure 'outsider' into their homes. Periodically the various leaders meet and are instructed by the pastor and share together their experiences. Mr Tucker readily admits that these house groups are one of the most effective methods the church utilises to contact and win the unbeliever. And if such an approach can be successful in this very difficult area of east London, one is led to believe it would work almost anywhere. All it takes is dedication and instructed lay people. And there is a wealth of material provided on how to conduct such groups.

Another fruitful field is the so-called all-age Bible

study. I have earlier referred to the Rev. Rodney Collins in the section on Christian education. He has built up a fine example of all-age Bible training in his pastorate. So committed is he to the value of this approach to an instructed congregation that he has tenaciously worked through many problems that such an undertaking naturally entails. His church buildings are far from the best. He has had a minimum of trained leadership flowing into his church. Financial resources are limited. All he really has is vision and determination. But that is enough! He is constantly training and helping leaders. He utilises his buildings in an imaginative way. Most buildings are far more flexible than one would at first guess and accommodations can be found outside church property if one looks about. But so convinced is Mr Collins that *everyone* needs Bible training, not just the children, that he has worked diligently for several years on the scheme. Now a fine programme of all-age Bible study is a regular part of the church's life. A short time back I shared a conference on all-age Bible training with him and he told me that after seven years they are now beginning to see real results from the long efforts that have been put into the plan. Again, one is tempted to say, if he can do it in his relatively small, limited church, anyone can. You do not have to have vast resources, just vision and determination.

Then, young people's work must be given a fresh look. One thing is certain in this field of ministry—conventional methodologies will reach few young people today. That is, young people whose families are totally unchurched. It is quite clear that church members, and especially youth leaders, must learn to accept young people as they are and let them express themselves in their own way; provided of course it is in line with Christian principles. If their music, dress and language are strange to the older generation, it does not necessarily mean they are wrong. And young people are open to the gospel in a fashion not experienced for many years. Young people are asking serious questions today. Let us be open, imaginative and zealous to reach them. If it takes unusual things to reach them, may the church be mature enough to employ such methods. And do let us be open and receptive to the 'Jesus People'. Much success has been had in this entire area by imaginative churches and their leaders.

The young men studying for the ministry at Spurgeon's Theological College where I teach have brought real innovations to churches where they have ministered to young people. They have found that two or three methods seem very effective at the moment. First, there is coffee-bar work. At the Holmesdale church in south London a group of our young men led the regular young people of the church into a coffee-bar programme. A room was found. It was 'decorated'—at least I suppose one could call it that. The rather drab old room was suddenly made alive with psychedelic walls and wild music. But when the church's young people got the word around the community that a coffee-bar was being held, the outside young people came in droves. This usually is the case. Often the problem is what to do with all those you attract. Our older men trained the church young people to witness and the results were that many from the outside came to find Christ. And the work is still going on. Surely, this is what evangelism is all about.

In the same geographical area of London, the men from Spurgeon's planned a gospel concert. Here is another real possibility for effective outreach. They rented a local civic hall—a neutral hall seems important for this kind of venture. Two Christian pop groups were enlisted from the Musical Gospel Outreach organisation. And word was put out in the area of what was to take place. Actually, tickets were sold. Young people today feel that if anything is worthwhile, you have to pay for it. The night of the concert saw the hall well filled with young people from all walks of life. As I sat there and heard the music, saw the clever skits that our men wrote and presented, and recognised that the gospel was genuinely being communicated, I realised you could never get that many young people into a regular church service to give them the good news in the conventional way. And any church can develop a gospel concert programme. If a pastor thinks he cannot, let him ask a few of his own young people. They will usually get the idea implemented. Many are just waiting for an opportunity to reach others in the ways they know are effective.

And, of course, what has been said previously about small groups has a very relevant application to young people. Time would fail to tell of the exciting things I have seen when young people are brought together as a group to learn more of Christ. Church after church is turning its younger members loose and letting them develop their groups. The church where I personally hold membership has one of the greatest groups of young people I have ever seen. And their programme centres largely around their own plans and schemes. But at the same time, they are well fused into the whole life of the church and support its entire programme well. The two are not in opposition to one another at all. And there are many young people who through this approach are reached for Christ.

Further, a geriatrics programme offers many opportunities. So many older people are isolated and lonely. Especially is this true in the larger metropolitan areas. They cry for recognition. A report was given on television recently that some older citizens are so cut off and alone that the only people they relate to are television personalities, and they will actually kiss the TV receiver when the face of their favourite appears. This should cause the Church to do some real heart-searching—and maybe some genuine repenting.

An interesting programme for senior citizens has been undertaken by the Sutton Baptist Church in London. They have actually erected a building of flats to house elderly, retired people. Seeing the pressing need for accommodation and a sense of belonging, the church ventured into this ambitious scheme and has successfully brought it into being. Financing is not the problem one might at first suppose. The monies can usually be secured and the programme remains solvent. It certainly does not require a wealthy church to undertake such a plan. And it is obviously a tremendous ministry to the elderly.

In my last pastorate we did several things for the older people of the community. Actually, those above sixty years of age formed the largest segment of the church. We discovered it takes so little to be of help to these people. And if you could see the joy and happiness one spreads by working with these folk, it certainly makes every effort worthwhile. Trips were planned for them. A regular visitation by the laymen was instituted. Social times at the church were a regular occurrence. A myriad of activities can be conceived. And these lonely people desperately need our love and care. Why could not almost any church develop a senior citizens club of its own? It would mean much to many and I am sure be used by God to reach people for Christ.

And, of course, every community has its own special peculiar needs. Delinquency, crime, dope, illegitimacy, minority groups, under-privileged areas, the isolated wealthy, needy sub-cultural groups, etc., all these and many other needs can be discovered. The local church should attempt to step into these gaps and minister. The Church must get involved in the life of the community. It has been provincial and insular too long. The world needs to know the Church exists and is there to minister.

One of the finest examples that I have discovered of late concerning a church that is ministering to the whole community is the Central Methodist Church in Wisbech. At a recent visit to this new work I was much impressed by their overall programme. They have had the advantage of new buildings, but that is not the real reason for their success. It is the spirit of adaptability and their sensitivity to community needs that has led them. They are located right in the heart of the main shopping district of their town. The church building itself looks much like a store front with a snack bar as the most prominent feature. Actually, the sanctuary of worship is on the top floor. The pastor, the Rev. F. W. Thixton, explained all they were doing to contact and minister to the community. First, they really do have a snack bar that is open to the public. Shoppers, people passing by, can come in, buy a cup of coffee or tea and eat a light snack. The furnishings are attractive and comfortable and a warm atmosphere prevails. This snack bar is open even on Sunday night and people come in, drink coffee and on the side they hear the worship service in progress above as it is piped down on a sound system. And, incidentally, the worship services are always alive and relevant. For example, the day I visited, a gospel pop group was rehearsing for the coming service. It is also significant that the pastor has his study right beside the snack bar. Of course, he does not push himself on people, but he is there and available every day. It is easy for people to see him. The value of this is obvious. Moreover, each day other parts of their building are open for a variety of ministries. There is a daily play group for children to help mothers who wish to leave their children for a period. There is a young wives' club that meets regularly. Youth activities are prominent. An excellent geriatrics work is beginning. A chiropodist, a hairdresser, etc. come in to minister to the elderly who frequent the place. Hand-crafts are developing. They plan soon to start serving very cheap meals for older people of the community. In a word, they are constantly expanding into new, exciting ways to meet needs. And it is clear why they are making the positive impact on the town that they are.

Of course, I realise they have much going for them in their new buildings that were designed with just such a programme in mind. But most church buildings are far more adaptable than we may suppose. A measure of redecorating and restructuring will often do wonders to old buildings. I further realise that such an ambitious undertaking means radical change for many congregations. But in the fenlands, where Wisbech is located, people are traditionally known for their conservatism. But here is a church that went ahead and is now doing a marvellous work.

Then there are the multiplied personal ministries the church members can be educated to perform. Personal witnessing is vital and expected of all. Most of us are aware that in the final analysis, personal witnessing is the most effective way to confront people with the gospel. Few unbelievers come to the church at this moment in our history. Therefore, it is the housewife witnessing to the shopkeeper, the worker speaking about Christ to his friends on the job, the young person giving the good news to school mates, who will help make an impact on contemporary society. If only God could open our mouths. On this theme, Wilson Carlile said, 'I have got the biggest job I have ever tackled in my life. I am trying to open the mouths of people in the pews'.[29] I am almost bold enough to say that either the mouths of God's people will be opened or we are done for. To use a play on words over Gavin Reid's book, we must stop 'gagging God' by our silence. Yet surely Christians can be inspired and helped and educated to share their witness.

An illustration of what one man can accomplish as a personal witness is the story of M. L. O'Neal. This man was the most effective witness for Christ I have ever personally known. He was not a pastor. He was a simple layman. He was not highly educated. Actually, he had to drop out of school at fourteen years of age to go to work to help support the family. He was not a great Bible scholar though he faithfully read his Bible. He was anything but a theologian. His speaking ability was not outstanding. Later in life he became a very successful business man. But this was not his genius. His most remarkable quality lay in his ability to lead others to faith in Christ. And this quality developed out of his ardent passion to win the unconverted. He seized every opportunity to witness. I have seen him bear his testimony in every conceivable context. He would witness to waitresses in restaurants, attendants at filling stations, clerks in stores; wherever he met people. I remember him driving thousands of miles just to witness for Christ. But so skilful was he that he rarely offended anyone. I know for a fact he led literally hundreds to faith in the Lord Jesus Christ. He actually burned out his life in seeking people. He became seriously ill not too long ago. An operation was mandatory. As he was being prepared for the surgery, he faithfully witnessed to the male nurse who was caring for him. He died a short time later—but what a way to go! His whole life was consumed with this one passion. I suppose a misunderstanding psychiatrist would say he was a compulsive or obsessive personality. But here was one layman, totally committed, and God used him significantly. Of course, I know few laymen will ever become that effective, but many can be led to do far more than they are now attempting. To this equipping the pastor must give himself.

It would further seem wise for members of the church to engage personally in community affairs. So often a caricature is drawn of the Christian as a rather isolated, strange, unreal character—especially is this true of the pastor. And I suppose this is not completely without some foundation in fact. A ghetto mentality has surely invaded segments of the Church. But if God's people get involved in community affairs (they are citizens of the country as well as of the Kingdom), this image can be altered and opportunity for outreach and Christian ministry found.

May I share a personal illustration of this principle? While serving a church as pastor near a large university, I became convinced I should involve myself in the life of the university. An entrée presented itself to work on several committees of the International Centre of the university. It was time-consuming and on occasions even inconvenient. It caused my wife and myself to curtail certain other activities that some would have felt more important. But we were thrown into contact with people outside the Church as never before. We had the opportunity of ministering to students, leaders and personalities from all over the world. And in this context we were able to bear our witness for Christ. A leader from a foreign, non-Christian country came to us on one occasion. We attempted to entertain him in a Christian hospitable manner. We tried to be a friend to him. We gave him a copy of the New Testament in simple, modern English. He visited our worship services. Before he left us, he had read a large portion of the New Testament and so impressed was he with the Christian warmth he had experienced among our church people, that he said, 'If ever missionaries from your churches want to come to our country, I shall let them in.' And he was in the position in his country to do that very thing. We must minister to the world whenever and however we can. We shall never reach people by being walled up in our cloisters.

Furthermore, there are countless opportunities to demonstrate Christ's love in deeds of kindness that Christians can be encouraged and helped to attempt. Wherever there is a need, a Christian can step in. As an example of this type of service I would like to tell of a dear lady in a former pastorate I held. She was very poor by many standards. Her husband was rather unstable. But she excelled in personally doing helpful things for people. She was never able to do big things—finances prohibited that. Yet she was always doing what she could. And she was loved and appreciated for it. Her spirit of genuine Christlikeness in meeting needs as best she could was inspirational. Surely Christians can be led to emulate this principle in their daily lives.

The list could go on. But let the mission action group along with the help of the entire congregation discover what God is leading the church to do, corporately and individually. God is in this world ministering; the church should be there with Him. Let us break out of the four walls of our buildings and meet the world. There is much material produced today to give direction on the suggestions made above and on other approaches as well. And surely the Holy Spirit will lead the church and its individual members into avenues of mission outreach that will prove effective for God's glory and the winning of men.

1. Michael Green, *Evangelism in the Early Church*, p. 173.

2. ibid., p. 175.

3. George Goyder, *The People's Church* (London, Hodder and Stoughton, 1966), p. 9.

4. Quoted in J. A. T. Robinson's work, *The Layman's Church*, p. 10.

5. John R. W. Stott, *One People* (London, Falcon Books, 1969), p. 24.

6. ibid., p. 47.

7. ibid., p. 47.

8. ibid., p. 54.

9. This and the following main points are from an unpublished paper given by Dr A. V. Washburn at the Baptist World Alliance Conference on Teaching and Training held in Tokyo, July 12–18, 1970.

10. Roger L. Shinn, *The Educational Mission of our Church* (Philadelphia, United Press, 1962), pp. 66–7.

11. A. Leonard Griffith, *What is a Christian?* (Nashville, Abingdon Press, 1961), pp. 117–20 (London, Lutterworth, 1962).

12. From an unpublished paper given by the Rev. Rodney Collins at the Baptist World Alliance Conference on Teaching and Training, Tokyo, 1970.

13. Alvin J. Lindgren, *Foundations for Purposeful Church Administration* (Nashville, Abingdon Press, 1965), p. 60.

14. Ordway Tead, *The Art of Administration* (New York, McGraw-Hill, 1951), p. 101.

15. Quoted from an unpublished paper given by the Rev. George Wilson, Jr. at the Baptist World Alliance Conference on Teaching and Training, Tokyo, 1970.

16. ibid.

17. *The Expositor's Bible*, 1 Corinthians (London, Hodder and Stoughton, 1891), p. 276 (italics mine).

18. *The International Critical Commentary*, 1 Corinthians (Edinburgh, T. & T. Clark), p. 264.

19. Alexander Rattray Hay, *The New Testament Order for Church and Missionary* (New Testament Missionary Union, 1947), p. 177 (italics mine).

20. *An American Commentary*, vol. v (Philadelphia, The American Baptist Publication Society, 1887), p. 104.

21. R. C. H. Lenski, *The Interpretation of St Paul's First and Second Epistles to the Corinthians* (Minneapolis, Augsburg Publishing House, 1937), pp. 496–7.

22. Alexander Rattray Hay, op. cit., p. 186.

23. *The Interpreter's Bible*, vol. 10 (Nashville, Abingdon Press, 1953), p. 164 (London, Nelson).

24. *The Expositor's Greek Testament*, vol. 2 (Grand Rapids, Erdman's Publishing Co., 1951), p. 887 (italics mine).

25. William Barclay, *Letters to the Corinthians*

Philadelphia : Westminster Press, 1954), p. 120 (Edinburgh, St Andrew Press, 1954).

26. R. C. H. Lenski, op. cit., p. 497.
27. William Barclay, op. cit., p. 124.
28. George Goyder, op. cit., p. 35.
29. Quoted in John R. W. Stott, *Our Guilty Silence* (London, Hodder and Stoughton, 1967), p. 13.

4

The Preaching of the Pastor-Evangelist

At a recent conference for theological teachers we heard a lecture from a professor of education on the inadequacies and serious shortcomings of the lecture method of teaching. After the rather paradoxical hour was over, one of my colleagues asked our lecturer privately if what he said about lecturing in the classroom applied to preaching in the church. The professor retorted that though he was a lay preacher and preached every Sunday, so convinced was he of the irrelevance of formally addressing people that he felt the one hour spent each Sunday listening to a sermon was virtually a waste of time.

What the distinguished professor of education felt concerning preaching is not an uncommon attitude today. Perhaps as never before in the history of the Church has the preaching enterprise been so seriously called into question. Douglas Stewart tells us :

> Preaching as such has fallen into disregard if not into disrepute. To localise this fact one could easily construct a historic chain of dominant London preachers from John Donne to Charles Haddon Spurgeon, who generation after generation, in their immensely varied traditions, shaped and influenced the life of London. But somewhere, between Spurgeon and ourselves, the chain is broken . . .[1]

Yet this is only to be expected, the antagonists of preaching declare. After all, their arguments run, is not this the 'post-Christian' era? Are we not in the television age? What is called for is something new if we are to grip men today. Forthright proclamation of the truth is out. Dialogue is now in vogue. The uneasy mind of modern man demands pictures, involvement, discussion, etc. In the light of such widespread feelings, it is small wonder that the Bishop of Bristol has said, '. . . preaching is in the doldrums, if not in the dog-house'.[2] A classic example of the current mood is seen in the fact that once the motto of Glasgow was 'Let Glasgow flourish through the preaching of the Word'. Today the same city has on its promotional material simply 'Let Glasgow flourish'. What has happened to the preaching of the Word?

Now if what has been said about preaching in general be true, it is especially applicable to evangelistic preaching in particular. Today, even from our own preaching ranks, many feel that 'preaching the gospel' as we traditionally understand that phrase is almost an exercise in futility. Why preach evangelistically to those who are already evangelised, it is often asked. Few, if any of those who need to hear the good news ever come to the church services, we are told. But such an attitude was far from the case until quite recent times.

The history of preaching
It is known to all that the preaching enterprise has an illustrious history. As far back as Old Testament times the preaching prophets stood head and shoulders above other men. Hear Elijah thundering out judgment upon Israel until even Ahab quaked! See the tearful Jeremiah preaching with such influence that finally Zedekiah permitted him to be cast into a pit in order to stop his voice! Or look at Elisha boldly addressing King Jehoram as he tells the monarch to send Naaman to him that all may know there is a prophet in Israel! And time fails one to

relate the thrilling stories that centre around the preaching of Amos, Isaiah, the mystical Ezekiel and their fellow-prophets. Viewing the old dispensation, one thing is certain and stands out in bold relief; the preaching of the prophets had a profound influence on every aspect of the Israelite nation.

The New Testament era makes no change in emphasis; preaching remained paramount. In fact, preaching came into its own in the apostolic age. Preaching in the early Church was central to the divine mission, and its impact upon its contemporary society was profoundly significant. Who could deny, for example, the influence of the preaching of John the Baptist upon Israel? All Jerusalem went out into the desert to hear him. Or look into the ministry of the Lord Himself. Ker has said that 'The great work of Christ during His life was preaching'.[3] Perhaps this is to overstate the case, but it is obvious that preaching was a very significant part of Jesus's ministry. Our Lord's own testimony of His life and ministry was that He came 'to bear witness to the truth' (John 18:37). It naturally follows, therefore, that the apostles and early disciples would fall into the same tradition. Whether it was Peter at Pentecost, Philip in Samaria or Paul in philosophical Athens, the power of proclamation was skilfully employed.

The Church fathers were no exception to the rule either. They were great preachers. One still marvels at the impact of men like Origen, Clement and others. And so it is through centuries of Church history. It was said of John Chrysostom that it were better for the sun not to rise on Constantinople than for Chrysostom to stop preaching. Even in the dark Middle Ages great preaching was not entirely lost. Bernard of Clairvaux was so persuasive in his sermons that it is reported mothers would lock their sons in the house to restrain them from following him back to the monastery. Francis of Assisi, though excelling in many Christian attributes, always considered himself first of all a preacher.[4]

But it is when we come into the Reformation period that we observe preaching blossoming out on a scale such as it had not done for many years. No one questions the fact that preaching was a vital and essential factor in this movement. Men like Luther, Calvin, Knox and others were not only great theologians and writers; they were also very convincing preachers. Had these men and their colleagues not been persuasive proclaimers of their doctrine, one wonders what would have become of the Reformation.

After the ministries of preachers like John Bunyan, the eighteenth century dawned and brought the advent of another era of great preaching. Wesley, Whitefield, Edwards, Zizendorf are still almost household words. Under God, as these men preached, spiritual awakenings occurred. The next century was little different except that this was the time of great pastoral preaching as well as an hour for the evangelists. Thousands flocked Sunday after Sunday to hear the oratory of pastors like Spurgeon, Dale, Clifford, Brooks, and Beecher. And simultaneously the revivalists were preaching to large crowds. Finney, Moody, Chapman, Torrey and a host of others won thousands, even millions, to Christ. And where would the modern missionary movement be if it were not for the great preachers of the eighteenth and nineteenth centuries, men like Carey, Judson, Rice, Taylor and their kin?

Even the twentieth century has not been bereft of effective preaching, despite the current disillusionment with the practice. Billy Sunday, notwithstanding his weaknesses, is credited with winning a million people to faith in Christ. And no man in Church history has preached to more people than our contemporary Billy Graham. Moreover, there are men of God this very day who are filling their churches with worshippers who come to hear the Word of God preached.

Thus, in the light of a long and significant history, I make bold to conclude that the days of proclamation are not forever past. That preaching is currently on bad times is true, but I am convinced a revival of effective preaching is not as unthinkable as some seem to imagine. I even believe evangelistic preaching can have a new day. I do not mean by this that we should retreat into the false security of living in the past. I certainly do not mean to imply we should disregard other modern methods of communication that technical progress has given us. Moreover, I know a methodology can hold for centuries and suddenly, because of a radical change in circumstances, become totally irrelevant. For example, since matches have become available, few people any longer rub sticks together to start a fire. And I am aware that some think preaching is like rubbing sticks. But I believe preaching can come alive in our day. Even in our empirical, existential, technological age, I feel preaching —yes, evangelistic preaching—can be effective. As we develop our 'go-structures', we can still find a very real place for the preaching of the gospel in the context of our church services. This I believe. It is not an 'either/or' choice of our 'going to them' or their 'coming to us'. It is development of *every* kind of evangelistic activity that we are calling for. But if we are to preach Christ effectively today, it demands a fresh look at the entire preaching enterprise.

The prerequisites of effective evangelistic preaching
Three things seem very necessary to communicative preaching today, especially to evangelistic preaching. If preaching is to regain its historical role, these principles appear vital. First, there is the consideration of the content of the proclamation. For evangelistic preaching to be successful, there must be a clear-cut positive presentation of the biblical meaning of the gospel. Secondly, there is the methodology. Here is where awareness to the preaching situation must be paramount. We must communicate to man in such a way that he will truly hear and act. Finally, there is the consideration of the

preacher himself. There must be some qualities about him as God's man if he is to preach with effect. Preaching is always the communication of 'divine truth *through personality*'.[5] Let us now look at these three principles in some detail.

The content of evangelistic preaching

Although one never appreciates the type of preaching that grows out of a bigoted and narrow dogmatism, there must be no 'uncertain sound' from the pulpit when the gospel is proclaimed. As Webster reminds us:

> A mood of uncertainty about the heart of the Gospel, the Lord of the Church, and the Saviour of the world, is unworthy of Christians and bodes ill for the future of missions if it is allowed to be encouraged or persists. Describing the first mission to Thessalonica St Paul wrote: 'When we brought you the gospel, we brought it not in mere words but in the power of the Holy Spirit, *and with strong conviction*, as you know well' (1 Thess. 1:5). Christian, even theological, humility is not synonymous with vagueness.[6]

What then is our message? What is that 'foolishness of the proclamation' (1 Cor. 1:21) that God uses to save men?

C. H. Dodd's approach to the kerygma

Ever since C. H. Dodd gave us his classic little volume *The Apostolic Preaching and its Development*, much interest has centred on the idea conveyed by the New Testament word *kerygma*. And its importance is patent, for in the term we seek to find the essence of the good news we are to preach. As Dodd approaches the subject he makes a quite unbending distinction between *kerygma* and *didaskein*. *Didaskein* he defines as teaching, i.e. largely ethical and moral instructions on the

Christian life. Occasionally, he tells us, it includes what we would today call apologetics. At other times *didaskein* contains theological doctrine, for example, in the Johannine writings. But all *didaskein*, Dodd implies, must be seen as quite different from *kerygma*. For *kerygma* is preaching; preaching of the nature of a 'public proclamation of Christianity to the non-Christian world'.[7] Thus Dodd concludes that in the light of this contention much of the preaching in the contemporary Church would not have been recognised by the early Christians as *kerygma*. What we hear in large measure on Sunday morning in many congregations is teaching or exhortation (*paraklusis*); a *homilia*, that is a discussion on the Christian life and thought directed to those who already believe.[8]

But to preach in the New Testament sense of the word, Dodd goes on to contend, has for its object—at least the great bulk of the time—the gospel of Jesus Christ. He holds that the basic idea contained in the term *keryssein* is so close to that conveyed by the word *evangelizesthai*, to evangelise, that for all practical purposes the terms can be used synonymously.[9] Thus he concludes:

> For the early church, then, to preach the Gospel was by no means the same thing as to deliver moral instruction or exhortation. While the church was concerned to hand on the teaching of the Lord, it was not by this that it made converts. It was by *kerygma*, says Paul, not by *didache*, that it pleased God to save men.[10]

What then is this primitive *kerygma*? What is the essence of our proclamation? Dodd's understanding of the essential *kerygma*, first in Paul's epistles, can be summarised in the following manner:

> The prophecies are fulfilled and the new age is inaugurated by the coming of Christ.

III

He was born of the seed of David.

He died according to the Scriptures, to deliver us out of the present evil age.

He was buried.

He rose on the third day according to the Scriptures.

He is exalted at the right hand of God, as Son of God and Lord of quick and dead.

He will come again as Judge and Saviour of men.[11]

Dodd grants that the preaching of Paul probably contained more than this, but it at least has the above as its basis for evangelising.

Moving on to consider the preaching of Peter and the others as found in Acts, Dodd discerns six basic elements in their *kerygma*. First, the age of fulfilment has dawned. The Messianic age has come (Acts 2:16). Secondly, this new age has taken place through the ministry, death and resurrection of Jesus Christ. And a brief account of this is *always* given. The concepts of the Davidic descent, the Lord's ministry, His vicarious death and His glorious resurrection are presented. Moreover, these truths are presented in the context of scriptural prophecy fulfilled as determined by the foreknowledge of God. Thirdly, by virtue of the resurrection, our Lord has been elevated to the right hand of God as Messianic head of the 'new Israel' (Acts 2:33–6). In the fourth place, the Holy Spirit is the sign of Christ's present power and glory (Acts 2:33). Fifthly, the Messianic age will shortly reach its consummation in the return of Christ (Acts 3:21). And lastly, the *kerygma* in Acts always closes with an appeal for repentance, the offer of forgiveness, the gift of the Holy Spirit and the assurance of salvation in the life of the 'age to come' (Acts 2:38–9). Thus, Dodd summarises, 'We may take it that this is what the author of Acts meant by "preaching the Kingdom of God".'[12]

A contrast between the Pauline proclamation and the Jerusalem *kerygma* makes it clear that Paul emphasised three things that are not as explicit in the preaching found in Acts. First, in Acts, Jesus is not normally called the 'Son of God'. His titles are more in line with the prophecies of Isaiah. But, of course, as Dodd states, the idea of Jesus as Son of God is deeply embodied in the Synoptic Gospels and these first three books of the New Testament were probably little influenced by Paul. So the preachers of Acts were surely not averse to the idea of Jesus as Son of God. Secondly, the Jerusalem *kerygma* as over against Paul's preaching does little in declaring that Christ died *for* our sins. As Dodd puts it, 'the result of the life, death, and resurrection of Christ is the forgiveness of sins, but the forgiveness is not *specifically* connected with His death.'[13] Thirdly, the Jerusalem *kerygma* does not emphatically assert that the ascended Lord intercedes for us as does Paul. But for the rest of the points in Paul's gospel, they are all found in the sermons in Acts.

Michael Green and the kerygma

Since the time Dodd wrote his classic the bookshelves of pastors' studies have been filled with volumes that build upon this essential thesis. Wide and varied have been the approaches as one surveys these works.[14] Questions on Dodd's approach have naturally been raised. Recently, for example, Michael Green has contended that 'there has been undue concentration on what has become technically known as the "*kerygma*" . . .'[15] He holds that Dodd and others may well have made the *kerygma* far too fixed. At one point he even raises the question as to whether or not there even was a fixed *kerygma*.[16] He contends that surely 'the probabilities of the situation would militate against undue fixity in the presentation of the message'.[17] What is to be seen, Green argues, is that the background and understanding of the listeners helped determine what aspect of the truth of Christ was preached. Green is not alone in this contention, for this is also the approach of Professor

C. F. D. Moule in his book *The Birth of the New Testament*. Edward Schweizer also writes along similar lines in an essay found in *Current Issues in New Testament Interpretation*. Perhaps the best full-scale treatment of this problem is found in R. C. Worley's work *Preaching and Teaching in the Early Church*. It must be recognised, Green tells us, that:

> It would be a mistake to assume from studies such as those of Dodd that there was a crippling uniformity about the proclamation of Christian truth in antiquity, that there was a basic homogeneity in what was preached we may agree, but there was wide variety in the way it was presented. Nor was this variety always the result of the supposedly rigid and conflicting theologies which were prevalent in different sections of the ancient Church. . . . But much of the variety will have been necessitated by the needs and understanding of the hearers. Evangelism is never proclamation in a vacuum; but always to people, and the message must be given in terms that make sense to them.[18]

Still, notwithstanding these valid comments, Green grants, as quoted above, that 'there was a basic homogeneity in what was preached'. What then is this 'basic homogeneity' as Green sees it? He contends that we shall not go far wrong in taking three basic points as essential to the Word the first-century Church preached.

First, they preached a person. Their message was frankly and unapologetically Christocentric. And this gospel message was not so much centred on His life and public ministry; rather, it was upon His death and glorious resurrection.

Green holds in the second place that the early Church proclaimed a gift. It was the gift of forgiveness, the gift of the Holy Spirit, the gift of adoption and of reconciliation. And that kind of grace made 'no people' the 'people of God'. Concerning this concept of a gift, the emphasis was placed upon the gift of forgiveness and the gift of the Holy Spirit.

Thirdly, the first-century Church looked for a response from their hearers. The apostles were anything but shy in asking men to decide then and there for or against Christ. They expected results—positive results. These early preachers declared men must do three things in the light of the gospel.

1. They must repent. This was first and foremost.

2. They must exercise faith. A continuing life of faith was called for, but it must begin by a 'leap of faith'. Of course, true faith is inseparable from repentance.

3. The apostles preached baptism. It was seen as the seal on God's offer of forgiveness and the essence of man's response to that offer in repentance and faith.[19]

Thus Green presents his understanding of the *kerygma*. And though there is probably genuine validity in his criticisms of Dodd's more inflexible approach, it is clear he also sees the essential proclamation in a definite, definable sense.

James Stewart and the kerygma

Another interesting writer on the theme of proclamation is James Stewart in his popular book *A Faith to Proclaim*. In this helpful volume he tells us that the first axiom of evangelism is that the evangelist must be sure of his message. However, he does not, on his own admission, attempt to traverse again the ground that Dodd, Oscar Cullman, Rudolf Otto and others have done in attempting to discover the primitive *kerygma*. His purpose is to find the bearing the *kerygma* has on present day questions. So from this pragmatic perspective he gives us what he feels is that essential proclamation.

> What, then, was the essence of this proclamation by the original heralds of the faith? Quite briefly it was this. They proclaimed that prophecy was

fulfilled; that in Jesus of Nazareth, in His words and deeds, His life and death and resurrection, the new age had arrived; that God had exalted Him, that He would come again as Judge, and that now was the day of salvation. This was the message.[20]

From the above statement Stewart derives five principles that should be found in all proclamation. First, the evangelist must declare the incarnation. The facts of the *kerygma* are historical facts. The doctrine of the incarnation means that 'God has come right into the midst of the tumult and the shouting of this world'.[21] But the facts of the incarnation are not only historic, they are unique. The Kingdom of God, no less, has broken into the here and now. And that is unique and unrepeatable, Stewart correctly concludes.

Secondly, the evangelist must proclaim forgiveness. And this is very relevant, for 'whenever the Church truly proclaims the forgiveness of sins there the healing ministry is veritably at work'.[22] The feeling of meaninglessness in life so relative to our existentially oriented society must be recognised as a problem of sin. Iniquity and rebellion against God are the ultimate culprits in the contemporary loss of direction, emptiness and feeling of utter aloneness. Therefore, as the Church preaches forgiveness it strikes right at the heart of many present-day problems. As Kierkegaard said, 'I must repent myself back into the family, into the clan, into the race, back to God'.[23]

In the third place, Stewart goes on to say the proclaimer preaches the cross. The veil has been rent; the veil which keeps men out of God's presence and that which shuts God in. The still darkness and mystery of God's 'wholly otherness' has now been flung open to men. Reality can be touched. As Stewart expresses it, 'The death of Christ gives me the very heart of the eternal, because it is not words at all, not even sublime prophetic utterance: it is an act, God's act, against which

116

I can batter all my doubts to pieces. We preach Christ crucified, God's truth revealed.'[24] But the death of Christ does not stop just at revelation. The apostolic *kerygma* goes much further. The cross speaks of atonement, guilt-bearing, expiation. Moreover, the demonic forces of the universe were once and for all defeated. Christ has overcome the world. 'We preach Christ crucified' is always to be the cry of the evangelist.

Fourthly, the 'hour cometh, *and now is*'. The new age, the long expected hope, has occurred. Christ has been raised. We preach a resurrected, living Lord. 'This is indeed the very core of the apostolic *kerygma*',[25] Stewart correctly states. It was the theme of every Christian sermon. The fact of the resurrection was no mere appendix tacked on the end of their proclamation, as it appears in some contemporary messages. The resurrection is a cosmic event. It is not just a personal victory for our Lord. All history was shattered by this creative act of God Almighty. The resurrection means that the whole world has died and a glorious rebirth has taken place. Nothing can ever be the same again. Naturally, the apostolic message did not see Good Friday and Easter as two isolated events. They were always presented as one individual mighty stroke of God. And now time has been baptised with eternity; things on this side immersed in things on the other. Moreover, there is no atonement and reconciliation apart from the resurrection. It is God's act of justification. 'This is our Gospel. For this is what Christianity essentially is—a religion of Resurrection.'[26]

Finally, and in summary, Stewart declares that the evangelist simply preaches Christ. The message is not a cold conceptualised theology or philosophy. A person is preached. And what a person He is; the helper, shepherd, companion, friend, light and bread of life, our paraclete. If Christianity is anything it is an experience of a 'vital relationship to a living Christ'.[27] This is the great discovery the world needs to make. How different contemporary society would become if it truly understood what this means.

Thus Stewart casts the *kerygma* in a pragmatic context. He applies all the essentials of the proclamation to living human situations. And surely this is what must be done in actual preaching. We must thoroughly understand our message theologically, but it must always be related in terms that addresses the *kerygma* to real life.

The kerygma in Douglas Webster

Douglas Webster in *Yes to Mission* points out the essence of his grasp of the *kerygma* in four basic principles. He begins his presentation by reminding us that 'mission implies that the Church does have something to say'.[28] Thus he states that evangelistic preaching must always centre upon :

1. The person and character of Jesus Christ. He really did live and was unique above all other men.

2. The teaching of Jesus Christ. He said things about God, life, the Kingdom of God and human destiny as no one had ever spoken before.

3. The death of Jesus Christ. The death of our Lord was the turning point in all history and God was ultimately active in it.

4. The resurrection of Jesus Christ. Death did not end it all for the Lord, rather it was the end of death, for He is a *living* Saviour.

Webster correctly points out that though some want to add more to the gospel than the above four essential points, it is certain that 'we cannot have less, if we are to retain the Gospel at all'.[29]

Now what is to be learned from these and other varied approaches to the *kerygma*? Two lessons seem vital. First, whether we take the more rigid view of men like Dodd or a more flexible approach like that of Green or Webster, there is still an essential and basic content to evangelistic proclamation if it is to be biblical in nature. There are certain theological and historical realities that must be clearly understood and declared in the presentation of the gospel. And it is clear that these basic truths centre in and around the person and work of Jesus Christ. Secondly, and to our immediate concern about preaching, it must be stressed—as already implied—that our evangelistic messages must contain the essential *kerygma* if we are to expect God's full blessings upon our preaching. So many evangelistic sermons today seem rather bereft of the real biblical content of the *kerygma*. Mere appeals to the imagination, emotions or what have you are not what the New Testament understands by preaching. 'We preach Christ'; this must be our theme in all our attempts to win men to Christ by preaching. I have a firm conviction that any preacher who aspires to preach the gospel must be very careful to have the essential content of the *kerygma* in all of his evangelistic messages.

The methodology of effective proclamation

As important and fundamental as the content of preaching is, it is not the whole story of effective proclamation. The proper preaching situation is vital to the success of evangelistic declaration. What I mean by the preaching situation is the entire setting of what transpires in a meaningful evangelistic preaching experience. It must always be remembered that the activity of preaching is not *merely* a means for conveying the content of the Christian faith. Preaching is a unique activity in the Christian context. It is an Event; an Event wherein God meets man. It is a form of God addressing Himself to man.

As H. H. Farmer has put it:

> . . . preaching is telling me something. But it is not merely *telling* me something. It is God actively probing me, challenging my will, calling me for decision, offering one His succour, through the only medium which the nature of His purpose permits

Him to use, the medium of a personal relationship. It is as though, to adopt the Apostle's words, 'God did beseech me by you.' It is God's 'I—thou' relationship with me carried on your 'I—thou' relationship with me, both together coming out of the heart of His saving purpose which is moving on through history to its consummation in His Kingdom.[30]

It is just here that the distinctive nature of effective evangelistic preaching appears. And this is why preaching can be seen in one sense as a sacrament. Preaching is only distinctively Christian preaching in so far as it is both uttered and listened to *in faith*. In other words, baffling as it may seem, preaching is God's activity, i.e. it is God encountering men in the extreme and supreme crises of their lives. Real preaching—*kerygma* or *didache*—utterly depends upon the preacher conveying the sense of the living, saving activity of God in Christ.[31]

Perhaps it should be said here that the distinction between *kerygma* and *didache* is not to imply that the two never blend. Nor should this distinction be understood as dictating methods of communication. The preacher in the pulpit can be in the context of *didache*. And a layman in dialogue with another can surely be in the spirit of proclamation. *Kerygma* is not to be understood as always a monologue, nor is *didache* always dialogue. It is communicating the truth in the method that the immediate situation calls for that is to be sought. And as emphasised above, declaring God's word is always to be done in faith and heard in faith. This implies, therefore, that all genuine Christian communication is something of a dialogue whether it be *kerygma* or *didache*.

Now the principles of Christian preaching imply a number of things. Initially, preaching must always be viewed as a personal encounter. God confronts people in the preaching situation on a Person-to-person level.

As Farmer expresses it, '. . . God's "I—thou" relationship with me is never apart from, is always in a measure carried by, my "I—thou" relationship with my fellows.'[32]

In the light of this truth it is possible to see the position in which this places the proclaimer. In the first place he must himself be intimately related to God in an 'I—thou' sense. If he loses the reality of God's presence in his preaching, all is lost. Then he must also be related to his hearers with genuine rapport in this 'I—thou' manner of understanding relationships. Actually, the preacher stands, as it were, at the corner of a right-angled triangle. He is related vertically to God and horizontally to his hearers in the preaching situation. In the context of this setting God completes the triangle and confronts and addresses man. Moreover, there is give and take in all directions on the triangle. It is an existential encounter *par excellence*. This is preaching.

Secondly, the immediate implication of the above concept is that preaching is costly. Effective proclamation does not come easy. The preacher is giving of himself. The relationship is of an 'I—thou' nature, not an 'I—it'. And that always costs. The proclaimer is pouring out himself to God on the vertical dimension and pouring out himself on the horizontal to the people. Thus he so gives of himself in the preaching experience that he is drained. Preaching can be painful when one gives of oneself as one ought. The pulpit is not a place to be cool and casual in spirit and attitude. It was Paul who said, 'Therefore be alert, remember that for three years I did not cease night and day to admonish everyone *with tears*' (Acts 20:31).

Thirdly, therefore, the preacher must keep people in his vision. As important as is the content of one's message, it is people that must be seen as central. We do not preach in a vacuum. We know, as already quoted from Stewart, that 'The evangelist must be sure of his message'. And perhaps in this age of uncertainty and relativity this is more important than ever; but preaching is *to people*. And it is to them we address our message in love, compassion and understanding as we attempt to relate to them meaningfully. And we speak to men in their life situation. Life situation preaching is a must these days. Thus we conclude that all other aspects of methodology are secondary to the basic existential preaching situation we have described. This the preacher should understand and attempt to cultivate. For this is the context in which God works.

The preacher himself

Finally, a word about the man who declares God's message is in order. Dr Raymond Brown reminds us that the effective preacher today must have three essential qualities.[33] He must first be an acute observer. It takes more than just understanding the Sciptures to be a preacher who is relevant to today's world. He must be a student of his contemporary society. He must know his world. The late D. T. Niles said, 'If we want to talk with God we had better find something about the world because that is the only subject in which God is interested.'[34] And the same surely is true if we want to speak *for God*. Roger Schutz has correctly confessed that often 'we allow ourselves to be caught up in a Christian environment that we find congenial and in the process create a ghetto of like-minded people who are quite unmindful of the real world'.[35] We must preach to real men in real life. But surely we have emphasised this principle enough.

Secondly, the preacher must be a compassionate listener. As Brown puts it, 'Before he talks he must learn again to listen'.[36] He must listen on a two-fold level; he must listen to God and he must listen to people. He speaks for God to the needs of people. And how can he effectively communicate unless he is genuinely open to both? We need to emulate the spirit of Ezekiel when he said, 'I sat where they sat and remained there astonished

122

among them.' It was there that the prophet learned to be God's spokesman.

In the third place, the preacher must be a discerning teacher. This we have already stressed most emphatically in the last chapter on the role of the pastor as one who builds up the church for mission. And, of course, the need is obvious. If ever there was a day of alarming ignorance concerning the Word of God, this is that day. May God make of His spokesmen those who are faithfully 'holding forth the Word of life' (Phil. 2 : 16).

Thus we can say by way of summary that the pastor-evangelist must be a man of God. He must be one who walks with God. He must know by experience—daily experience—the One for whom he speaks. As Farmer has well said, 'I suppose in the end the secret lies in the quality of our own spiritual life and the extent to which we are ourselves walking humbly with God in Christ.'[37] But we shall have more to say about this in the last chapter.

As we now come to the final section on the theme of preaching the gospel, may we look into

The evangelistic service

There is perhaps some legitimacy in raising the question as to whether we should attempt today to have evangelistic services in our churches. There was a time when it was quite common, but as we well know many today doubt its validity. Of course, it is clear by now that I believe it can and should be attempted. I find myself in substantial agreement with Farmer when he says, 'I, for one, . . . believe that there can be no substitute for the sermon, and I have little sympathy with the tendency in some quarters today to minimise it, and even to suggest we might get rid of it altogether.'[38]

But why this current reluctance to have a regular evangelistic service, whether on Sunday or at a special time? Why is there a disillusionment about conducting evangelistic services today? Several misconceptions or problems seem responsible for tending to make our pulpit evangelism less effective and thus have contributed to this general disillusionment with its value. First, some pastors have been hesitant in giving a whole service over to evangelism because of the relatively few unbelievers who seemingly normally attend. But the obvious answer to this problem is that there are *some* there. And these, if only a few, need to hear the gospel preached. Moreover, there may well be more unbelievers attending than we realise. Just because practically all present are church members, this does not assure us all are truly regenerate believers. Billy Graham said that in America the greatest evangelistic opportunity is in the churches themselves. And I doubt that it is much different elsewhere. Furthermore, I simply believe that if pastors will faithfully develop good evangelistic services from time to time and forthrightly preach the gospel, the Holy Spirit will honour the effort and bring unbelievers along to hear the good news. True, I cannot even proof-text that statement, but experience and observation verify it for me at any rate.

A second problem is that some pastors tend to restrict their pulpit evangelism to just a short word of encouragement to accept Christ at the end of almost any kind of sermon or service. This practice is far from that which gets positive results. It is no substitute for real proclamation as we have attempted to define the idea. The whole service needs to be shaped and geared to the aim of winning people to Christ if it is to be decidedly and effectively evangelistic.

Then, there are preachers who for one reason or another fail to give a definite challenge to the unbeliever. Thus they see little result and are disillusioned with preaching evangelistically. But this practice is to make the error of preaching only part of the *kerygma*, i.e. they may preach all about the Christ Event but fail to remember that the apostolic message called men then and there to repent and believe. As John Stott has expressed it, '. . . we must never make the proclamation without then issuing an appeal'.[39] I have often wondered, in the light of this principle, why some pastors will not give some sort of challenge or invitation. Could it be because of the fear of failing to generate a response? Well, the response is not up to us. That is between the unbeliever and God. Ours is merely to challenge and help, theirs is to respond. Perhaps the reluctance simply grows out of timidity. But we are to be strong in the Lord. We have no reputation to keep or build as Christ's ambassadors. We simply do His bidding. We represent Him. I suppose some refuse to issue an invitation because of theological convictions. But the New Testament itself is ample justification for extending a call to accept Christ openly. Of course, the type of invitation given should be of the nature that suits the situation. No one method suffices for all contexts. But surely the Holy Spirit can guide His ministers in how to do it. It is the failure to be so guided that I think so often robs our pulpit evangelism of much power.

However, perhaps the prime reason why some pastors view the evangelistic service as ineffective today is because they feel inadequate and/or uninstructed on just how to develop a sound, sane and spiritual evangelistic thrust in the context of a service. Of course, none of us feel expert in this. In such a high and holy venture, who does feel competent? But perhaps a few suggestions here can help us all as we aspire to win men to Christ through preaching.

Simple principles for the evangelistic service
Let the preacher first of all have real confidence in the fact that, as Sweazey states, 'His pulpit still offers the minister his supreme evangelistic opportunity. No form of communication the Church has ever found compares with preaching.'[40] Now even if Sweazey has overstated the case, it is still evident that the evangelistic preaching service has an important role in mission. Let us have

confidence that God can and will use this methodology. Thus a number of disciplines must be followed.

First and foremost, there should be adequate preparation. This must be seen in a two-fold sense. Initially, the minister must be fully prepared himself. This includes spiritual, mental and emotional preparation. He will want to open the service with his sermon not only well in mind, but with the assurance that it is the essence of the *kerygma* and that his basic objective is to win people to faith in Christ. Then he will want to be prepared spiritually so that in faith he can fully expect God to bless the preaching of the gospel. And his enthusiasm should be evident to all. This mental, spiritual and emotional preparation does not come in a few moments. It is costly. Moreover, preparation for an evangelistic service means preparing the people as well as preparing oneself as the preacher. I think it a fine approach on occasion to inform the church in some fashion that an evangelistic service is planned for a certain date. Enlist the people to pray, to invite unbelieving friends and then to come expecting God to bless and to draw people to Himself. The more that is put into such a service, the more we have a right to expect God to honour it. But just to decide on Saturday, because a gospel sermon has not been preached lately, that Sunday is the time to preach evangelistically is a far cry from the kind of preparation needed.

Then, it is vitally important that the proper atmosphere be developed in the actual service itself. Of course, this is essentially the work of the Holy Spirit. But there are a number of instrumental things that God can use to create such an atmosphere. First, there should be something of a positive dynamic about the entire service. There should be a positive spirit of joy. We are proclaiming the *good* news. The spirit of warmth, expectation and joy that God's people exude is most helpful and provoking in itself. A number of things go into helping create this. Let me mention a few that may at first sound a bit negative. I think it is a time for relatively short prayers. There is, to be sure, a time for longer prayers, but the evangelistic service is not the time to pray for too many things. The unbeliever will just not follow it. Long periods of announcements are not helpful. Further, the man who conducts the service should not be sombre and slow. The whole service should move along smoothly and reasonably rapidly. The right music is obviously vital. Ideas concerning church music need a drastic updating in most of our congregations. How the world feels about music in the churches was brought home to me a short time back by an article that appeared in a large London newspaper. It bears reading. It went as follows:

> Millions of children still rise to their feet at nine o'clock every morning to sing a hymn. Ask them at eleven o'clock what it was about, and all they can remember is the number. Dragging tunes, incomprehensible words about fountains of blood, abasement, sin—what effect do these have? Has the result of hymns been to corrupt poetic taste, destroy musical interest, and to lump religion in children's minds with the feel of gulped porridge and a hastily-scrubbed face?
>
> Innovations like 'pop' hymns merely immerse the old splurge ('Tread underfoot our ghostly foe, That no pollution we may know') in a *Salad Days* sauce (Beguine tempo). Genuine attempts to redeem poetic and musical meaning make only slow progress.

We are not to let the world dictate to us our methodologies, yet this should give the pastor something to reflect upon. And it seems clear that the music in an evangelistic service can almost make or break its effectiveness. As Edwin NcNeely states, 'It has been said many times that religion must "sing or die", for "music . . . with its inherent emotional content, becomes a powerful force in drawing men into a proper relationship with God".'[41] Thus the hymns chosen should present the gospel in a positve, enjoyable and singable fashion. And let's be up to date in all selections, at least as much as possible. The time is overdue for hymns based on the language of an industrial, urbanised society rather than a rural nostalgia. One would hope that God would raise up hymn writers who can communicate the true message of Christ in the words and phrases that are meaningful to today's mentality and thought structures. Here is an area for much thought and prayer. I do not intend to imply that all the older hymns are passé. It is interesting that the very day I write this the radio in London has reported that the number five tune in the pop charts this week is John Newton's *Amazing Grace*. Still, an updating in most hymnology is urgently called for. Further, I feel special music can be employed most effectively. Choirs, soloists, groups, instrumentalists can and should be skilfully employed. Parker said, 'I believe that there is as much conviction lodged in the mind by singing as by preaching'.[42] It is wise, therefore, for the preacher to give serious, imaginative attention to the music phase of the service.

Thirdly, in developing an effective evangelistic service, little probably needs to be said about the actual preaching itself. This we have already discussed in some detail. Perhaps the word of Blackwood concerning evangelistic preaching is enough here. He states, 'As for the preaching, every sermon ought to glow. It should be a burning message from the heart of God to the man in the pew.'[43] But again do let me emphasise the importance of extending an appeal. In most instances (though I should not wish to make this an unbending rule), after a warm evangelistic sermon, some sort of opportunity for a response from the people in the pew should be presented. This must, of course, be guided by the Holy Spirit. Surely He can lead and inspire His preacher what to do. Some years ago Faris D. Whitesell produced a book entitled

Sixty-Five Ways to Give Evangelistic Invitations. He correctly makes the point in this book that the whole impact of evangelistic preaching 'reaches a logical climax in the appeal'.[44] The sermon should move towards such a goal. And surely if one preacher can conceive of sixty-five ways to extend an appeal, under God a few and relevant means of issuing an invitation can be found. Whether it be to step out publicly on the spot, to come to the minister's vestry after the benediction, to ask for prayer or by any other means; the issue is that we give some kind of appeal in most circumstances. And the preacher must not fear the results. The minister is not a 'success' or 'failure' according to the response.

Finally, it seems wise to involve lay people in such a service. Testimonies, special music, etc. can often be skilfully employed and project the image that the service is really of and for the people. This obviously helps break down many barriers.

In a word, the preacher must be imaginative in creating an evangelistic service. And when a creative, dynamic service is developed and the gospel is preached in the power of the Holy Spirit, I believe God will honour it. A short time ago I was conducting a service in a church in Coventry. The entire hour was given to evangelism. The good news of Christ was presented in song, prayer, sermon and spirit. After the benediction I made my way directly to the minister's vestry with the challenge left to the people to follow Christ in commitment and faith and to those who would so decide to come to the vestry for prayer and counsel. One of those who responded was a young man in his early twenties. His words to me were few, but very profound. He simply said, 'I want you to know I really met God in the service this morning.' As long as that keeps happening today, I for one will keep preaching the gospel and challenging people to come to Christ. As the poet put it :

Give us a watchword for this hour,
A thrilling word, a word of power,
A battle-cry, a flaming breath
That calls to conquest or to death.
A word to rouse the Church from rest
To heed her Master's high request.
The call is given, you hosts arise,
Our watchword is evangelise.

1. From an unpublished address 'Preaching Today' by Dr Raymond Brown delivered at Spurgeon's College, London in 1969.

2. ibid.,

3. John Ker, *Lectures on the History of Preaching* (London, Hodder and Stoughton), p. 33.

4. Andrew W. Blackwood, *The Preparation of Sermons* (New York, Abingdon-Cokesbury Press, 1948), p. 15 (London, Church Book Room Press).

5. ibid., p. 13 (italics mine).

6. Douglas Webster, *Yes to Mission* (London, S.C.M. Press Ltd., 1966), p. 20.

7. C. H. Dodd, *The Apostolic Preaching and its Development* (London, Hodder and Stoughton, 1936), p. 7.

8. ibid., p. 78.

9. ibid., p. 8.

10. ibid., p. 8.

11. ibid., p. 17.

12. ibid., p. 24.

13. ibid., p. 25 (italics mine).

14. Michael Green, *Evangelism in the Early Church*, p. 61.

15. ibid., p. 48 (italics mine).

16. ibid., p. 60.

17. ibid., p. 61.

18. ibid., p. 115.

19. ibid., p. 150–2.

20. James S. Stewart, *A Faith to Proclaim* (New York, Charles Scribner's Sons, 1953), p. 14–15 (London, Hodder and Stoughton).

21. ibid., p. 18.

22. ibid., p. 50.

23. ibid., p. 55.

24. ibid., p. 82.

25. ibid., p. 104.

26. ibid., p. 110.

27. ibid., p. 143.

28. Douglas Webster, op. cit., p. 18.

29. ibid., p. 19.

30. Herbert H. Farmer, *The Servant of the Word* (London, Nesbit, 1941), pp. 27–8.

31. ibid., p. 30.

32. ibid., p. 56.

33. Raymond Brown, op. cit.

34. ibid.

35. ibid.

36. ibid.

37. H. H. Farmer, op. cit., p. 90.

38. ibid., p. 81.

39. John R. W. Stott, *The Preacher's Portrait* (London, Tyndale Press, 1961), p. 50.

40. George E. Sweazey, *Effective Evangelism: The Greatest Work in the World* (New York, Harper and Row, 1953), p. 159.

41. Edwin McNeely, *Evangelistic Music* (Fort Worth, Seminary Hill Press, 1959), pp. 4–5.

42. As quoted by Edwin McNeely, ibid., p. 3.

43. Andrew W. Blackwood, *Evangelism in the Home Church* (New York, Abingdon-Cokesbury Press, 1952), p. 129.

44. Faris D. Whitsell, *65 Ways to Give Evangelistic Invitations* (Grand Rapids, Zondervan, 1955), p. 11.

5

Obstacles to Effective Evangelism

It may appear slightly repetitive to give an entire chapter to the obstacles a church faces as it engages in mission. Many of the current problems the evangelistically-minded pastor and church face have already been mentioned. Yet it seems appropriate to discuss in some detail certain paramount issues and then to attack them positively in the hope that some guidelines to a solution can be found.

The modern problem of communication
Perhaps the most complex issue to be confronted at this hour is the modern problem of communication. I say modern, because its seriousness is being felt today as probably never before in Church history. Despite the complexity of the problem the obstacle it actually presents to mission can be stated quite simply : How do we communicate the good news of Christ to great masses of society which virtually pass the Church by as though it did not exist? In other words, how do we get the ear of modern, technologically-oriented man?

But why, we are prone to ask, should the quandary of communication be such a stinging issue today? Do we not have means of communication at our disposal that the Church has never had before? What has precipitated the situation? In answer to this basic question it must first be understood that the essential nature of the problem is not as one would perhaps superficially suppose. What I mean by that is this: it is quite easy to see the quandary as one of language, vocabulary, failure to use modern aids, and so on. These are problems, to be sure, but they are only secondary. Words and ideas are not the big hang up in the communication tangle. The basic difficulty is sociological. In recent years factors in the very fabric of society itself have so altered the essential nature of our western sociological structures that communication has become an extremely difficult problem for all. Perhaps a cursory survey of the past few centuries will help us to see this in relief.

Ever since man has existed, he has lived in something of a tribal context. For millenniums society was structured around a close-knit community to which man could belong. These communities were great sources of security because of their inter-dependent nature. The members of the tribe fished, hunted, worked, farmed together. Even their recreation was in a spirit of togetherness. One truly belonged. This community type of living provided man with a very viable society. Now with this kind of social structure, it is obvious that communication was no problem. As a matter of fact, tribal man could scarcely breathe without the whole community knowing and discussing it. His life was a shared life. He shared his ideas, his experiences, his very self with those of the community. He communicated with his fellows on a real depth level.

But approximately five hundred years ago—a very recent time in the light of man's complete history—a crack in the community dyke appeared. The printing press came on the scene. The coming of the printed book began to change radically the entire structure of how the average man could receive information and knowledge. Before Gutenberg only the elect few could have a library. But now all potentially had the possibility of reading. And how does a man normally read a book? Alone! Hence we see the beginnings of the modern rise of individualism. The steps toward an atomic society began.

Then the industrial revolution began to break on the horizon in the western world. And this was more than a mere crack in the dyke. A veritable avalanche of social change swept across society and all but drowned community life as it had been known for ages. Invention followed invention. Factories to produce the fruits of the revolution mushroomed. People moved by the millions from their old communities to the rapidly growing urban areas. Moreover, the new residential areas into which they moved were so diverse that their neighbours were not necessarily their work-mates, their helpers in the communities, or hardly even acquaintances. To this were added long working hours and/or time-consuming travel. And the movement grew and grew as isolationism deepened until consequently, as Gavin Reed states, '. . . men have in fact become non-community animals'.[1]

One further step was needed, however, to complete the breakdown of community. Many people still met in groups outside the work-shop, for example in the pub, the working-man's club, the gardening groups, *the church*. But then the technical revolution began to dawn and the step was taken. Television, radio and the mass-media put recreation and communication right into the home. Man no longer needed his social group. Leisure time could now be well spent inside the four walls of his own castle; the home.

Thus community broke down in the great urban crush of the exploding metropolitan areas. Of course, there are still the remnants of real community here and there in the western world. There are yet the small villages that have some form of communal life. Also, there are the pubs and social groups that centre around some hobby or profession. But these tend to be very definite 'in groups' with their own life style and esoteric vocabulary. Moreover, they normally consist of a quite narrow, restricted peer group and a ghetto mentality usually persists. Tragically, one can also view the Church very similarly. But the fact is that in western Europe and the U.S.A. over 80 per cent of the population live in urbanised, industrialised areas where community to a large extent has been obliterated. And if the prophetic sociologists are right, that number will go up to well over 90 per cent in not too many years. In summary, we must just face the fact that community as man has known it for millenniums is gone.

Now what does all this mean? It is simple: *when community broke down, so did communication.* Where there is no communal or tribal circle, how does one talk in depth to others? This is an acute problem for every facet of society. The business man feels it; how can he get his product or service before people? The psychiatrist knows it only too well. Emotional illness due to isolation and failure to relate in depth to people is abounding. It is a *desperate* problem for the local church. For if we cannot communicate to the masses, how do we get their attention to give them the good news of Jesus Christ? I hope we as Christians can feel the depth of this disturbing issue. It is deadly serious for the contemporary local church. Actually, the Church feels it more acutely than other aspects of society. The mentally ill either go or are sent to the psychiatrist. The business man can solve his promotional problem by the use of mass communication. He can, for example, advertise on television or in the newspapers. But what about the Church? Society does not compel spiritually ill people to go to church. And in most of Europe it is almost impossible to get any kind of a foothold in the mass-media world. Although this is not quite the case in America, it surely is in many parts of the world. Moreover, it may well be an increasing problem in America before many years.*

* It is also true that in America community has not broken down to the extent it has in Europe. After all, Europe is seventy-five years senior in the industrial revolution. But all the trends in America are in that direction.

Of course, some have seen urbanisation with the attending breakdown of community as a blessing. At last, they say, we can be alone and live our own lives without the gossip or interference of others. But the cost of this perverted kind of privacy is a high price to pay. With it we have lost a sense of belonging and with that the important feelings of security. Thus we now fail to communicate in any depth to our fellows except to a very few family members and close friends. And here is just where the Church feels the crunch.

Now where does all of this lead? First, we must recognise that the Church has a problem on its hands that it has never quite had before. As Reid points out, 'It shows . . . that we do not start with the advantages of the Old Testament prophet, or of a New Testament apostle or even of a John Wesley. One thing was common to them all—they spoke to real communities and to community-man.'[2] Today the Church is simply not talking to men in community. And, tragically, it seems many Christians have not realised this fact. Our Church programming is often still geared to people as if they were yet living in community with a tribal or rural mentality.

Secondly, we must become vividly awake to the seriousness of this issue. I think Reid is absolutely correct when he says:

> The greatest threat to the gospel today in our Western industrial societies is not communism, apathy, humanism, impurity of doctrine or worldly compromise. It is this breakdown of communication not only from the Church to those outside, but also a breakdown of communications in every field of daily life. Unless Christians can find ways of saying things to modern non-community men then not only is modern man in a desperate plight, and not only is the Church facing extinction, but Almighty God Himself is gagged.[3]

Moreover, the problem is probably going to get worse. The present-day metropolis is giving way to the huge megalopolis. Knowledgeable sociologists inform us that what remnants we have left of community will all but be swallowed up in the new gigantic area-cities that will stretch for hundreds of miles. Therefore, again to quote Reid, 'We must not be surprised or downhearted if our towns and communities fail to show corporate responses to the gospel.'[4] It will be logistically almost impossible for them to do so.

Thirdly, it thus becomes patently clear that the old structures of church life that depended on speaking to men in community are over as far as their effectiveness is concerned. This, at least as I see it, is one of the big problems with our current local church life. And this is one of the reasons I have advocated so strenuously the overhaul of many of our contemporary structures.

The whole problem for the Church is obviously very complex and deep-seated. One is almost tempted to ask if anything can be done. But perhaps the picture is not quite as dark as may at first appear. I think there is one thing the Church can do that can be of real significance. Now if it has been the breakdown of community that has precipitated our failure in communications, and if the mass-media are largely closed to us, why can we not simply recreate community? If we could do this, we could communicate the gospel in that recreated community. This, I think, is the principle we must grasp if we are to solve our thorny problem. Of course, I know we cannot recreate the social, tribal community as it once was. We cannot turn back the sociological clock. These great movements are certainly beyond us. I do not mean that at all when I speak of recreating community. What I mean is this; why not build little 'communities' through the lives of the church members? Each Christian could become the centre of a 'mini-community', as it were. Actually, they already are in one sense. Everyone has his sphere of community, if it is only a few family members and friends. But why could not this circle become enlarged and developed into a sphere of Christian influence and Christian community? If members of the Church could be enlightened to see this and then be led and equipped to build a community around themselves, here would be a tremendous outlet for communicating the gospel. After all, is not this the principle behind the house group, personal evangelism, the all-age Bible study group, etc.? Actually, this is what we were trying to say in the concept of the lay-centred ministry. And I think it is perhaps the most intelligent and relevant way to approach the ministry in the local church in our age.

Such an approach will mean, obviously, that we cannot rely on what we do within the four walls of our church buildings to be the only or perhaps even our main evangelistic thrust. Moreover, it means we must release our members from the million and one 'church activities' so they can get on with building their 'community' wherein they can communicate Christ. This seems very important. And it further means that the church, the pastor in particular, must help to equip Christians for the task. We have already said much about this. But there it is; the breakdown in community and hence communication met by a new community through which Christ can be proclaimed. This, as I see it, is our hope for communicating the gospel today— and surely for tomorrow.

Now it may be helpful to say a few words about the secondary problems of communications mentioned earlier before we move on to the next obstacle to mission. Firstly, there is the problem of language. The criticisms are quite true that with our inward-looking churches we have developed something of an 'in-language'. Our vocabularies must sound rather strange, if not unintelligible, to the modern secularised outsider. It may well be that the 'language of Zion' was once communicative to the man in the street. But that is certainly not true today—especially to the younger generations. Actually, we are back to square one with the problem of the first-century Church. They had to learn to use a common idiom to convey their message. So must we. Thus we are in good company as we attempt to face our difficulties.

Granted, to update our religious language is not easy. Old speech patterns and emotive words—emotive to us, that is—do not change easily. But we must attempt to proclaim the good news in a vocabulary that is understandable to the average man. It is true that we have many good theological words that are very descriptive and we sometimes grope to find a better term. Thus it is legitimate to ask if we can ever completely escape all of our technical nomenclature? Or, would it even be helpful to do so? What then is the best approach? Well, some words we normally use are, I should suppose, the best we can find. Moreover, a certain amount of technical terminology is inescapable in any field, look for example at the scientific world. Thus the best course seems to be that we should use as simple a vocabulary as possible; then, when a term must be employed that we think the outsider will not fully grasp, we should take ample time to define and explain and illustrate its meaning in words and pictures he will understand. Surely this is what the apostles and early preachers did with the *koine* Greek. If we work at it, it is not too difficult to communicate our message in terms that are understandable. The point is that we become conscious of the problem and diligently work on it. For example, a short time back I had an opportunity to conduct a series of evangelistic services in Prague. There were attenders who were completely outside the Church. They lived in a completely secular, even atheistic society. The translator was not extremely fluent in English either. Thus I had an external circumstance thrust on me that forced me to take the above approach. I had to be very careful in the choice of many words, but I found that by keeping in mind the centrality of communicating Christ, and working on a simple vocabulary, people could quite easily get the message. Now if we can always see ourselves in at least something of a comparable situation, we should be able to declare Christ intelligibly to all our hearers. And, incidentally, when we preach or speak let us at all costs avoid that off-putting 'moral', 'ministerial' tone of voice. That intonation communicates all right, but not what we desire to communicate.

There is another aspect of the problem of communication that needs serious attention, namely the philosophical problem of epistemology. That is, what is the source and meaning of truth? In Chapter 1 we briefly discussed the issue. There we attempted to point out the spirit of relativism concerning truth that prevails in the thinking of many. *All truth* is somewhat relative, they would tell us. And this way of thinking has to some extent influenced much of the younger generation. Subjectivism is the criterion of truth for many today. Therefore, dogmatic pronouncements are frowned upon. Moreover, empiricism and rationalism have all but won the day in our scientific and philosophical circles, not to speak of their influence on the man in the street. Thus spiritual concepts seem meaningless to many because they cannot be verified by sense perception. And when we talk about concepts that transcend rationalism, they think us nonsensical. Now if we Christians are not aware of this climate and move to meet it, many will reject our message which is by its very nature positive and spiritual and at times above mere rationalism. Thus there is a call for an apologetic system that will meet the demands of this hour. Space forbids any such ambitious attempt here, but perhaps a few simple suggestions will afford some directions. Let us first recognise that any apologetic must be on a pre-suppositional level, i.e. we must 'argue' from a pre-suppositional epistemological basis. Secondly, help can be found in the works of men like Francis Schaeffer, Bernard Ramm, C. A. Campbell,

Rudolph Otto, and others. There are many good writings in this field. Let us remember we do not have to take an intellectual back seat because we believe the Bible to be the truth of God. Finally, we must never forget that it is our responsibility to 'always be prepared to make a defence to anyone who calls you to account for the hope that is in you' (Pet. 3 : 1). But after all is said, in the final analysis, it is the Spirit of God who convicts, convinces and converts the unbeliever. As we thus without any dilution or shame simply present the *kerygma* positively and forthrightly, God will honour it. Moreover, it is often a moral problem more than an intellectual one that keeps people from Christ (John 3 : 20–1). Honest intellectual difficulties can normally be met by the sincere knowledgeable Christian.

Further, the present day calls for a fresh look at the relevance of dialogue in communicating our faith. In Reuel L. Howe's significant work, *The Miracle of Dialogue*, he makes the point that dialogue is more than a mere method of communication, it is communication itself. It can effect depth relationships which are so vital to sharing one's faith. The wise minister will see that this principle is a real part of his life, service and ministry. Surely, he will want to guide his people into the principles of dialogue. Is not this really the heart of what we call personal evangelism? If Christians do not relate in real depth to people, how can they win the unbeliever? Furthermore, the church life itself should be structured in such a way as to allow for this type of interplay. People—at least young people—are moving away from a 'come sit and listen' mentality. Many want to be heard. No longer can we ignore this growing sentiment if we want to communicate to today's world.

By the same token, the group method must be exploited for effective communication. A minister must learn the principles of group dynamics. But we have already said enough about that.

In the last place, concerning the problems of

communication, it is surely wise to use all the modern means that are at our disposal. Audio-visual aids can be very helpfully employed. And as much as one can break into the mass-media, radio, television, print, etc., we should surely do so. It is difficult, I realise, but I have a pastor friend in the north of England who persistently kept after the local radio officials until he was finally put in charge of a regular religious programme. So perhaps more can be accomplished than we sometimes think if we are imaginative and tenacious.

Now, fundamental and complex as is the communication dilemma, there is another very serious issue the Church currently faces in its attempt to evangelise. Quite rapidly we seem to be polarising between a 'social action' approach to ministry and a purely evangelistic thrust. To this increasingly important problem we need to give a moment of attention.

The problem of social action versus 'frontier pietism'
The conflict between what was once known as the social gospel and the advocates of evangelism pure and simple, 'frontier pietism' as Gibson Winter calls it, is obviously nothing new. It has taken on a quite new complexion of late, however, in the advent of what is commonly termed 'secularisation' theology. The old social gospel of a few decades ago has by and large given way to secularisation thought. It is here where the battle is shaping up today. These secular theologians—or 'radical' thinkers as they are sometimes termed—are considerably diverse in their approach and in the depth of their radical orientation. John Macquarrie discerns three basic complexions in this New Theology. First, there is that school typified by Paul Van Buren in his book *The Secular Meaning of the Gospel*. In this work Van Buren maintains that it is impossible to believe in any reality apart from that which is open to empirical investigation. Thus for Van Buren 'secular' must be understood as excluding any kind of transcendent reality. It is obvious, therefore, where this

leaves traditional Christian theology. Quite correctly Macquarrie states:

> Thus Van Buren asked for what he called a 'reduction' in Christian theology, so that its content might be brought entirely within the sphere of the secular. This 'reduction' turns out to be a pretty severe mutilation of the traditional faith, for it means in effect that God Himself is to be left out. Van Buren's views are to be counted as belonging to the school that is trying to reconstruct Christianity without God...[5]

And, obviously, it is here that the radical death of God theologians find their home. Concerning this theological fad, of all the death of God thinkers, none are quite as exciting as Altizer. He alone raises the most fundamental problems for theology and the philosophy of religion. For to a greater or lesser degree, the other thinkers of the school like Van Buren are more or less traditional atheists. Thus they can be dealt with philosophically on that level. But not so Altizer. He really seems to mean that God once actually lived and then genuinely died. This is new. As Colin Lyas declares, 'It is because Altizer means what he says to be taken literally that he is the really interesting and disturbing death of God theologian.'[6] Again, space precludes a discussion of Altizer's position, but an excellent examination is found in Lyas' article 'On the Coherence of Christian Atheism' (*Philosophy*, January 1970, Vol. XLV, No. 171).

Another approach to secular theology can be typified in Ronald G. Smith's work *Secular Christianity*. Smith's basic orientation is an existential understanding of history, i.e. he tends to follow the Bultmanian approach and interprets the New Testament in existential and historical terms. Thus we have a brand of secularity that lays stress on the temporal and historical but does not proclaim the death of God and thus eliminate His transcendent nature.

Finally, there is the sociological turn to the New Theology as seen in the well known book of Harvey Cox, *The Secular City*. In this work, as Macquarrie points out, Cox '. . . shows no special interest in either empiricism or existentialism . . . [but] lets his thought be guided by sociological rather than philosophical considerations.'[7] Following Gogarten and others, Cox takes very seriously the secular mood of our time and regards secularisation as the natural outgrowth of the Christian doctrine of creation. Cox holds that we are to look to God and co-operate with Him in secular history. And of course, this means in the sociological structures and revolutions of our generation.

Thus within these three general categories most of the secularisation thinkers rest. Perhaps it would be best now to look in a bit more depth at the basic ideas of one of these men who have been quite influential, Gibson Winter. A clear statement of his position is found in his work *The New Creation as Metropolis*.

Initially it must be understood that Winter and his colleagues are not anti-mission. The converse is much nearer to the truth—mission is central to their theology. The Church must become the 'servant Church', he tells us. And, 'amid the disunity and secularism of the city, the Church is the ministering servant of judgment and hope.'[8] Moreover, the laity must be seen as the agents who are to fulfil the *missio Dei*. Winter says, 'A laity, theologically self-conscious and socially alert, is the form through which the Church's witness in metropolitan society will be realised.'[9] To this point, one can find little disagreement with his principles. The rub comes, however, when we begin to discover what Winter means by mission. It is certainly not what we have traditionally understood as the evangelistic task. This is illustrated by his rather sharp criticism of pietism in general and Billy Graham in particular. He denounces pietism by stating that, 'The piety of an individualistic frontier subverts the Gospel in an emerging metropolis.'[10] Furthermore, he goes on to say, 'Pietism replaces servanthood in the moment of metropolitan crises, disillusioning those who had looked to the churches for some direction in this hour of social class and racial conflict . . .'[11] Thus he clearly rejects pietistic theology, which has no doubt been a very basic influence in evangelism in the western world for many years—and which, I would be prepared to argue, is essentially rooted in the Scriptures themselves. As Winter therefore rejects pietism, it is not surprising to hear him speak of the Graham crusades in these words:

> The crusades divert Christians from the real task of the Church in the metropolis. They distort the Gospel, the Church and the character of the struggle to which the churches are summoned. The Graham crusade fosters pietism in place of servanthood. The Graham crusade uses the techniques of mass society to perpetuate the individualistic piety of the frontier. . . .[12]

In the light of the above quotation it would not be very difficult to conclude what he would say about much of the evangelistic effort we see in evangelical circles today.

Well then, what is mission according to Winter? In a word, what is the *missio Dei*? In answer to this central query, Winter first makes a distinction between secularisation and secularism. The differentiation is often made by this school. We have already seen this in Harvey Cox's approach discussed briefly in Chapter 1. Secularism is idolatry, Winter tells us. It can be seen in all spheres; political, educational, even in the religious realm. In the religious life, secularism 'is the substitution of religious structures and authorities for the Gospel'.[13] We can see it, Winter contends, in the struggle between religion and evolution in the last century,[14] dogmatism about the

Bible or particular 'facts' recorded in biblical testimony,[15] dualism in the contemporary Church[16] and
the current restriction of the religious life to the private
sphere of the inner emotional life and intimate relationships.[17] Now, of course, these things most Christians
would deplore. But two questions must be asked: (1)
Does Winter think all Evangelicals with a pietistic
orientation are guilty of such an approach to the Christian faith? Surely he knows this is far from the case?
Such a caricature is hardly fair. (2) Is the term 'secularism' the best term to use for such perversions of true
Christianity that Winter lists? Why not use the simple
old biblical word 'worldliness', for that is what it is
and I see no reason why it is not still a good word to
use as long as a definition is given. It surely communicates as well or better than 'secularism'.

But it is in the term 'secularisation' that Winter presents his whole idea concerning the *missio Dei*, and
consequently that to which the Church must give itself.
It is Winter's contention that what God is really doing
in the world in the secularisation process is the bringing
about of what he calls 'metropolis'. And it is in this context, this 'new situation',[18] that God's people are to find
themselves involved because here is where God is involved. What then is this metropolis that God is usher-
ing in through the secularisation process? Winter defines
it in these words:

> Metropolis is the possibility of a unified, human
> society arising from the chaos of our massive, ur-
> banised areas. . . . Metropolis is the realisation of
> unity of life out of the conflicting factions which
> now plague metropolitan areas. Metropolis is the
> fulfilment of the oneness of mankind out of the
> division of races and classes that now disrupts the
> metropolitan areas of our country. Metropolis is
> the human society which different groups subvert
> and which all groups need for their well-being.

Metropolis is the power of the New Mankind re-
fracted through human history.[19]

Winter thus concludes, 'To speak of metropolis, therefore, is to look with hope upon this metropolitan
conflict; it is to see the Church in her vocation for
humanity.'[20]

This concept obviously implies a number of things.
First, if God is at work *essentially* in the bringing about
of a new unity and harmony in the urbanisation process, He may very well be far more active in the office of
social security than in the local church. Secondly, the
Church fulfils its primary role in engaging as a reconciling agent in this unifying, sociological process. Thirdly,
what is meant by the term 'metropolis' is apparently
all but synonymous with what we have traditionally
meant by the Kingdom of God. Finally, the fact of the
atonement must seemingly be understood basically in
this sociological sense. And this is obviously of profound
significance. Clearly, this is a 'new theology'. This is
quite different from the old social gospel. This is radical
theology indeed.

Now perhaps one may think that these theological
speculations of the secularisation thinkers are restricted
to the proverbial ivory tower and are scarcely ever
worked out in the heat of an actual mission situation.
But this is not so. Many ministers seriously attempt to
implement these principles into their understanding of
outreach. For example, in a recent article in *The Baptist
Quarterly* of the British Baptist Union an industrial chap-
lain laid out what he saw as the goal of his mission to
men in industry. The secularisation approach in the
article was patent and his reliance on Gibson Winter
admitted. The author's understanding of the aims of
industrial mission read as follows:

To be present in industry and to understand it.
To stimulate responsible and critical thinking and

to encourage and support those who carry responsibilities.

To see the industrial situation in the light of a Christian understanding of things, and to do whatever may become possible there to help in the process of the word becoming flesh.

To report back to the Church, not only on what is happening out there, but also on the insights this work has found to be important.

To set up the kind of flexible structure that will serve these objectives.[21]

He goes on to say that much traditional evangelism today is mainly born of 'fear and despair' and is classified as 'tub-thumping' and 'bonhomie'.[22]

Now there are several things that disturb one about such an orientation to mission. But first, a positive word or two is in order. I think it applaudable that the secularisation concept of mission sees man as a social creature and attempts to speak to him in that context. It is no doubt true that pietism and much current evangelism has been lacking in its realisation of the fact that man is a gregarious creature. Perhaps individualism has been over-stressed at the expense of communal concerns in pietistic theology. Many Evangelicals need to learn more profoundly the meaning of the community of believers. Moreover, it is important to know that God is actually at work in the great sociological movements of our time and that the full work of the Holy Spirit cannot be restricted to just what He is doing in and through the instrumentality of the Church. God *is* at work in the office of social security. Cox is quite right to take a fresh look at the doctrine of creation—Evangelicals should as well.

But other questions arise—negative ones. Winter and his kin severely criticise those whom he sees as polarised on the individualistic aspects of the Christian experience. But after all, Jesus did come to save men individually as well as to put right the whole creation which travails until it is put right (Rom. 8 : 19–20.) We shall do well to remember what Bryan Green tells us when he says, 'no task is more important or sacred than leading an individual soul into personal conversion.'[23]

But why have Winter and these thinkers put themselves in this stance? They too are polarised. Could it be because of what they understand by 'metropolis'? This seems the crux of the matter. As already pointed out, Winter seems to equate metropolis with the Kingdom of God. Well, I suppose in one sense this is true. God *is* King over all. But Winter does not mean that.* He seems to see the emerging metropolis and all that it implies as the main work of God. Thus it is here, apparently, that the atonement is essentially at work—not in the individual as traditional orthodoxy has always contended. In other words, Winter seems to be constantly implying that it is to straighten out the sociological tangle in the rapidly urbanising world where the concept of reconciliation finds its primary meaning. This is what God is really doing. Or put it this way, individual conversion is out; communal or sociological conversion is in. And because this is what God is about, this is where the Church is to be involved in ministry. By ministering as the servant Church to mitigate the problems of poverty, racial strife, class distinctions, ignorance and fear, and so on, we are fulfilling our basic mission. If he does not mean this, he should have made it clear.

Now what can we say to all this? First, as important and worthy as social work is for the Church, Winter's theology seems to ignore totally all the Scriptures have to say about individual conversion. This we have already stressed. But it needs to be further emphasised that the New Testament seems so clear and obvious on the point

* To be fair to Winter, it must be made clear that he does not equate metropolis with all that one finds in the metropolitan areas of the western world. If I understand him properly, metropolis is an ordered, unified, harmonious entity within the city. And he sees it as emerging in the urban areas of the world.

of the necessity of individual conversion that a defence in this limited space is hardly necessary. I realise this implies that I have pre-supposed the complete authority of the Scriptures. But I do make just such a pre-supposition. Furthermore, I am convinced such a pre-supposition is far more defendable than that which the secularisation men apparently take. (We all do have our basic pre-suppositions.) Furthermore, if I may quote from my article written in reply to the paper on the aims of industrial mission in *The Baptist Quarterly* :

> . . . I am of the opinion that in the very depth of his personality, man is really asking, though usually quite unknown to himself, that old question of the Philippian jailer, 'Sirs, what must I do to be saved?' Though he would rarely express it in these words today, the human heart still longs for God. After all, we are in His image and made for Him. And although a man may seek to fill the 'God vacuum' in his life in a thousand different ways, he still longs implicitly to know the fellowship of his creator. This I firmly hold, on theological *and* practical psychological grounds. Thus when we answer man's deepest question on how to find meaning and reality in life through Christ, it is indeed good news that we share with him.[24]

Could it be that the basic error of Winter and others is that they are assuming a strange new brand of universalism concerning man's need of personal conversion? Now we must grant that God is surely uniting all things. But the Scriptures make it clear that He is uniting things in Christ (Eph. 1:9–10). But if *all* men are somehow already in Christ, thus precluding the necessity of personal conversion, and the atonement is to be seen as essentially applying to sociological structures, then Winter has a real point. In other words, if man does not need converting, and if what Christ did in the atonement is to be seen sociologically, then by all means let us give our whole selves to the building of a grandiose brotherhood of men by sociological and political ministries and it is all right if we call the product metropolis. But such a universalism is an assumption I cannot bring myself to embrace. I have already admitted my presupposition concerning the authority of the New Testament and I, for myself at least, do not find in the Scriptures any theology that comes in line with this kind of universalism. Therefore, if secularisation thought actually does assume a universalism, I must reject its understanding of the *missio Dei*. I just cannot equate Winter's metropolis with what I understand as the Kingdom of God or the 'New Jerusalem'. Nor can I identify the 'new mankind' of Winter with the 'fellowship of the saints' that the New Testament presents. Citizenship in the New Jerusalem and a place among the fellowship of the saints comes through personal repentance toward God and faith in our Lord Jesus Christ (Acts 20:21). And this is the basic truth—not the *only* one, but the *basic* one—the Church is to proclaim and is thus the foundation of all evangelism.

But does this mean that God is not at work in the social structures of society? Again I say no! Of course God is at work in all that is for the good of man. This is the kind of God He is. And if God is involved in the sociological milieu of mankind, so must be His Church. Let us do all we can to better the lot of our fellows. Let us work for all people regardless of who they are or what their need. This we must do if we are to be faithful to our Christian calling. But why be polarised on the meaning of ministry? Why let anyone, secularisationists or pietists, thrust us into an 'either/or' situation. It is not *either* social action *or* individual conversion to which we are to give ourselves, it is both. Thus if a man is hungry, we feed him; if he is sick, we heal him; if he is oppressed, we unite to free him. Moreover, I know that we live in such a social structure today that, as

Rutenber states, if we are to help the contemporary man who 'falls among thieves' on today's Jericho Road, we shall probaby have to form an action group and call ourselves the committee to make the Jericho Road a safe motorway. But by the same token, if a man is individually lost without Christ, we also meet that need by confronting him with the good news. And if I meet some social need of man I am not necessarily a 'social gospeller', nor if I attempt to lead someone to faith in Christ am I necessarily a 'tub-thumper' engaging in a gospel perversion called 'frontier pietism'. What is so difficult about this relationship between declaring the gospel and social action? Why is the balance seemingly so difficult to keep? Why all of this polarisation tendency? Actually, the relationship seems quite simple; we just find man where he is and in his need—whatever it may be, social, physical, mental, spiritual or what have you—and in the name of Christ step in to meet that need. As James Leo Garrett has well said, 'The crux of the present argument is that both evangelism and social involvement are essential to the mission and obedience of Christians today . . . the "both/and" stance is to be taken rather than either of the "either/or" stances. . . .'[25] I hope this is not over-simplifying that which is obviously a knotty problem for many. But in principle, I think it is that straightforward, and perhaps some have made more of a problem and obstacle of it than it actually is. A well rounded New Testament theology can surely motivate us to minister in God's purpose and will which is simply to find man in his multitude of needs and in the name of Christ meet those needs.

But now let us move on to consider an impediment to mission that is perhaps at least *felt* more keenly by the average pastor than any other obstacle, namely :

The problem of the apathetic church
A description of this obstacle to effective evangelism needs no elaboration. We all know it only too well.

Many church members are clearly 'God's Frozen People' to use Gibb's and Morton's phrase. How and when will the average Christian awake to his mission responsibility? It is even difficult to discern what has precipitated the current spirit of lethargy. Of course, there are several obvious partial reasons for the present spirit in many churches. There has been a lack of genuine worship with its vitalising influences. The problem of rooting Christians in a knowledge of the Scriptures has no doubt contributed to a lackadaisical attitude towards the things of God. I have already attempted to make clear the importance of a local church understanding its role in the *missio Dei*. Even a lack of leadership training has probably been a negative influence. But regardless of these and many other reasons, one thing is certain, a spirit of apathy has settled upon the churches in Europe and places elsewhere that is profoundly serious. All ministers battle with this problem.

What can be done to effect the spiritual awakening that we all desire to see so that the fires of evangelism may burn again? In principle, the answer is found in a work by C. William Fisher. He reminds us that 'Evangelism is really the outflow and the overflow of a spiritually vigorous church. Evangelism is the glow of an inner warmth, and the go of an inner compulsion. . . . Evangelism is not the cause but the result of a spiritual church.'[26] If one agrees with the above statement, the issue ultimately becomes, how does one make a church spiritual?

In answer to this basic query, at the very outset it must of course be said that one just does not *make* a church spiritual. This is God's work through the Holy Spirit. Moreover, to attack such a big theme in a few words is almost presumptuous. But perhaps a few things should be said merely by way of suggestion that may be of some value. The Holy Spirit does use means to effect a spiritual awakening, and if we can learn what some of these means are, we can at least make ourselves open to what He desires to do. I do not mean by this to restrict in any sense what God will do to effect the revival we need. He will do as He will. But at the same time the Spirit of God has moved in the light of certain principles in the past. These we can discuss.

First, God has promised to bless and use the communication of His word. But that teaching and preaching of the truth must have certain ingredients. It must be prophetic, i.e. the Word of God must be positively and forthrightly declared with a relevance to the human situation and needs as they are today. We currently hear much emphasis on prophetic preaching; and rightly so, for 'thus says the Lord' is what people desperately need to understand. Then, the pastor should communicate the message with a challenge. As I teach young preachers the rudiments of homiletics, I always strive to get them to see the necessity of a pointed object or aim in every sermon. And a real part of that aim is to motivate people into action. This demands challenge, and this element is often lacking in contemporary preaching. I am not asking merely for a 'hard sell' approach. But I am saying we must 'sell' no matter how we do it. We are to preach to move people to Christ. We preach for decisions. Good exposition is not enough. We need an element of exhortation in most of our ministries. As James tells us, we are not to be mere hearers of the word, but doers (Jas. 1:22). The preacher must always communicate the message with that principle and goal in mind.

Further, the problem of apathy can perhaps be somewhat mitigated by attempting to correct those things that I previously mentioned as some of the causes. We should strive to revitalise worship. We should keep the purpose and role of the Church before our people. We should help train leadership. And as already stressed, we should do all we can to get Christians rooted and grounded in the Scriptures.

But I suppose that in the final analysis we are just

about shut up to prayer and faith. If our churches are lethargic about the evangelistic task and in need of awakening, let us pray and pray and trust God to revive His work in the midst of years (Hab. 3:2). That which we so desperately need, namely spiritual awakening, comes essentially through prayer. And we who are leaders in the Church may need to pray first for ourselves that the quickening may begin in us. Then when our own hearts burn, let us start working with those of like spirit. It may be only one or two at the start, but that kind of fire God can spread. Perhaps we have made a mistake oftentimes in attempting to involve the whole Church in everything. It may be a very small remnant through which God will send His blessings. Let us work and pray with those who are open for all that God has and trust Him to open up other lives as well. Now granted, the above suggestions do not seem very exhaustive to meet such a pressing issue as apathy. But I must be frank, I do not know of any short cut to spiritual renewal. Yet, the signs seem to be multiplying that God is at work in marvellous ways among His people. Therefore, we can and should take courage in the Lord. Renewal may be on its way.

We now move to the final problem to be discussed.

Conserving the results
Every pastor has experienced the disappointment of seeing a person make a profession of faith, carry on for a time and then seemingly fall away. How do we meet this situation and conserve the results of our evangelistic endeavours? Well, it must be realised that Jesus Himself said that some of the seed would fall on shallow ground and would endure for only a short time and bring forth no lasting fruit. Yet this fact must not be used as an escape mechanism to avoid doing all one can to conserve the results of evangelism. May I therefore present a few simple guidelines.

Initially, there must be a proper presentation of the

gospel itself. That goes without saying. We must be careful to avoid ministering in such a way that our new converts stand in man's wisdom rather than in the power of God (1 Cor. 2:5). But given that, a proper philosophy of new member orientation is then called for. Often in classes or groups where new inquirers are taught, a basic mistake is made. It seems that through the curriculum new converts are at times given far more instruction on how to be a good church member than they are on how to be a good Christian. In other words, more effort is spent on integrating them into the structures of the local church than into the basics of the spiritual experience itself. And as important for Christian growth as the local church is, the prime need of the new convert is to learn the great disciplines and doctrines of the Christian experience.

Now there are at least seven points, it seems to me, that should form the foundation of new Christian orientation:

1. A rooting and grounding in the salvation experience. The new convert must know he is in Christ and secure.

2. An overall grasp of the great doctrines of the faith. Such a basic orientation seems essential for his understanding of all that transpires in his Christian experience.

3. An understanding of what the Bible is and how to read it profitably. The new babe in Christ is to desire the sincere milk of the word that he may grow thereby. (1 Pet. 2:3).

4. A basic primer on prayer. If one is to be strong in Christ, one *must* learn how to pray.

5. A grasp on how to achieve victory in trials, temptations and testings. In Christ there is victory and the new Christian must learn how to be an overcomer.

6. The meaning and place of the local church in one's life. This is obviously a very important part of orientation into Christianity.

7. The necessity of witnessing and service. The new

157

Christian needs to understand how to begin a life of witness and service for Christ.

If a new convert and church member gets established in these seven areas, he stands a far better chance, it would seem, to carry on in his Christian life. If proper materials to teach the above principles are unobtainable, let the pastor write and produce his own.

Another profitable programme that many churches have used with success is the assignment of 'shepherds' to the new members. Let one or more be responsible for the nurture, care and guarding of the young 'sheep'. Of course, these so-called shepherds must be mature themselves and will need to be trained for the task. And some administration for such a programme is called for.

Finally, the pastor himself will do all in his power to be a guardian of the whole flock—particularly new sheep. Every minister knows his responsibility here and the imaginative pastor can find a myriad of ways to help the new convert grow.

There are problems that impede evangelism to be sure. Many we have not even touched upon. But the pastor and Christian worker must remember that no problem is greater than God. And if God is in this mission enterprise we have been talking about, solutions and success can be found. The pastor has marvellous resources to be a victor in this battle. It is to a consideration of these resources we now turn in the final chapter.

1. Gavin Reid, *The Gagging of God* (London, Hodder and Stoughton, 1969), pp. 20–1.

2. ibid., p. 22.

3. ibid., p. 17.

4. ibid., p. 23.

5. John Macquarrie, *God and Secularity* (Philadelphia, Westminster Press, 1967), pp. 21-2 (London, Lutterworth).

6. Colin Lyas, 'On the Coherence of Christian Atheism' from *Philosophy*, January 1970, vol. XLV, No. 171, p. 8.

7. John Macquarrie, op. cit., p. 25.

8. Gibson Winter, *The New Creation as Metropolis* (New York, The Macmillan Company, 1963), p. 54.

9. ibid., p. 11.

10. ibid., p. 25.

11. ibid., p. 18.

12. ibid., p. 17.

13. ibid., p. 43.

14. ibid., p. 44.

15. ibid., p. 45.

16. ibid., p. 46.

17. ibid., p. 47.

18. ibid., p. 2.

19. ibid., pp. 2-3.

20. ibid., p. 5.

21. R. P. Taylor, 'Industrial Mission' from the *Baptist Quarterly*, January 1969, vol. XXIII, No. 1, p. 13.

22. ibid., p. 1.

23. Bryan Green, *The Practice of Evangelism* (London, Hodder and Stoughton, 1951), p. 149.

24. Lewis A. Drummond, 'What is the Goal of Industrial Mission', from *The Baptist Quarterly*, July 1969, vol. XXIII, No. 3, p. 109.

25. James Leo Garrett, Jr., 'Evangelism and Social Involvement', from *South Western Journal of Theology*, Spring 1970, vol. XII, No. 2, p. 60.

26. C. William Fisher, *The Time is Now* (Kansas City, Beacon Hill Press, 1950), p. 69.

6

The Resources and Power for Effective Evangelism

This final brief chapter may well be something of an epilogue to our appeal for evangelism. In these closing pages I wish us to see there is power to labour successfully in mission. Resources are available upon which the pastor-evangelist or any Christian can call that will enable him to make a significant impact for Christ and His gospel. And simply put, that is what the *missio Dei* is all about. Let us then first consider:

The power of a holy life
When one's service and ministry are finally summed up, that which makes the most lasting and vital impression is a Christ-like life. As a young minister, I once had the opportunity of serving as an associate pastor to a true 'man of God'—and I do not use that term lightly. This man was not the pastor of a large, influential church. He was not an outstanding or eloquent preacher. His intellectual achievements were not extraordinary. Yet his ministry was felt over a large area. Many came to faith in Christ through his witness. The one fact of his ministry that was so outstanding and that which gave him such influence for Christ in his community was the simple godliness of his life. And though he passed on some years ago, the man's impact still remains.

A number of things are implied by the principal

ingredient in the above account. In the first place, the image of the pastor-evangelist in the community is extremely relevant to the effectiveness of his ministry. As Gavin Reid has pointed out in his work on Christian communications, 'Image communication can have an important *supporting* role to play.'[1] Of course, this is true for any Christian, pastor or layman. Paul recognised that it is vital to be able to say of one's self, 'Brethren, join in imitating me, and mark those who so live as you have an example in us' (Phil. 3:17). When a man can honestly make such a statement, his life will prove powerful in mission.

Secondly, one's native ability is not necessarily the determining factor in an effective evangelistic ministry. It is obvious, of course, that God uses the talents we have, but as long as one's life is totally committed to Christ, God will make that life useful in mission—one talent or ten. And remember, He gives everyone 'gifts'.

Finally, it is important for all who aspire to be instrumental in evangelism to learn the principles of godly living. These principles are few and elemental. The entire concept can be summarised as simply knowing God in the experiential fellowship of Jesus Christ. As John in his first epistle puts it:

> That which was from the beginning, which we have heard, which we have seen with our eyes, which we have looked upon and touched with our hands, concerning the word of life—the life was made manifest, and we saw it, and testify to it, and proclaim to you the eternal life which was made manifest to us—that which we have seen and heard we proclaim also to you, so that you may have fellowship with us; and our fellowship is with the Father and with his Son Jesus Christ. And we are writing this that our joy may be complete. This is the message we have heard from him and proclaim to you, that God is light and in him is no darkness at all . . .

if we walk in the light, as he is in the light, we have
fellowship with one another, and the blood of Jesus
his Son cleanses us from all sin (1 John 1 : 1-5, 7).

It is quite evident from the above passage that daily
fellowship with Christ—walking in the light as He is in
the light—is the essence of living the kind of holy life by
which one genuinely knows God. Perhaps this foundational idea can be illustrated by an experience in the life
of a young minister who, as the story goes, had much
admired the ministry of an aged man of God who was to
bring an address in his city. The young minister, thinking that perhaps he could discover some secret that would
unravel the mystery of the tremendous success of the
old minister, went to the service seeking that which
would give him the insight to a similarly effective ministry. As it happened, however, when the time of the
service arrived, the old preacher, though present, was
not well and it was impossible for him to deliver his
message. The convener of the meeting, none the less,
prevailed upon the elderly gentleman to say just a word.
As the old servant came to the podium it seemed as
though the presence of Christ settled down on the entire
congregation. He then made one, simple statement. He
said, 'I'm glad that I know God.' These words fell like a
hammer on the young minister. 'That's it,' he exclaimed
to himself. 'That's his secret. This man truly *knows* God.'
And most would agree that the young minister made
a correct analysis of the situation. If our lives are to be
effective and successful as God counts success; if we
are to make the impact upon our communities and our
world that God intends for us to make; if we are to experience genuine renewal in our lives and in our
churches; we must come into a living knowledge and
true fellowship with God Himself. In a word, we must
come to know God, vitally and dynamically.

Now several things need to be said concerning the
possibility of knowing God in the sense of living daily in

His presence. Initially, it needs to be understood that as John saw it, Christianity was not a speculative system of thought nor simply a mystical experience. It was a mysticism of genuine communion with God as revealed objectively in His Son Jesus Christ.

Secondly, John views fellowship with God as a marvel. It is marvellous because of the fact that 'God is light and in him is no darkness at all' (v. 5). The metaphor concerning the character of God as 'light' is used in various places in the New Testament. This concept of light obviously refers to God's holiness, and from the various New Testament passages where this picture is drawn we can grasp something of the marvel of what it means to walk with God in the light. First, God is complete light. John has put it this way: 'In Him is no darkness at all.' In other words, God is completely and unequivocally morally perfect. His righteousness is infinite and ultimate. He is absolute holiness. God is light—complete light—and in Him is no darkness at all.

Moreover, not only is the light that surrounds the Godhead infinite and ultimate, it is also unchangeable light. James wrote, 'Every good endowment and every perfect gift is from above, coming down from the Father of light with whom there is no variation or shadow due to change' (Jas. 1:17). How different we creatures are. We change; the moral and spiritual tone of our personalities can go from the heights to the depths. But God's holiness is utterly unchanging. He can always be experienced as 'the same yesterday, today and forever' (Heb. 13:8). He is always perfect, unchangeable light.

Finally, Paul states in 1 Timothy 6:15–16 that God's holiness is unapproachable light. 'The King of Kings and Lord of Lords . . . alone has immortality and dwells in unapproachable light, whom no man has ever seen or can see. To him be honour and eternal dominion. Amen.' No doubt a new appreciation of the holiness, sovereignty and majesty of the God of light is a needed contemporary concept. The current humanistic overtones about

God as 'the man upstairs' or the sentimentalism that states 'somebody up there likes you' brings the God of holiness down to a level that is not found in the Scriptures. A fresh vision of the glory of God like that Ezekiel received—even in Chaldea where one would not expect it—is a real need, for when the prophet saw God for who He actually was, he fell on his face in the dust (Ezek. 1:28). We must never forget that God is light and His holiness is utterly unapproachable by sinful man in the flesh. Though He is intimate and concerned for us all, He is absolutely holy.

Now this is what makes the possibility of fellowship with God the wonder it is. God is light and we are darkness; the very antithesis of light. We hardly need be reminded that we are often found walking in sin's darkness. Yet, in spite of it all, we can actually walk in the light. And that is a marvel. How can it be?

Fellowship through confession
Fellowship with God is a glorious possibility. A holy life is conceivable. Yet it must obviously be worked out in the practical sphere of everyday living if it is to have any dynamic in one's experience. Foundational to the pragmatic implementation of the experience is the realisation that fellowship begins with *confession*. John tells us:

> If we say we have fellowship with him while we walk in darkness, we lie and do not live according to the truth; but if we walk in the light, as he is in the light, we have fellowship with one another, and the blood of Jesus and his Son cleanses us from all sin. If we say we have no sin, we deceive ourselves, and the truth is not in us. *If we confess our sins,* he is faithful and just, and will forgive our sins and cleanse us from all unrighteousness (1 John 1:6–9).

From the historical perspective, as we all know, John

164

was dealing with the error of the Gnostic concept that human flesh was sinful in itself. The Gnostics further erroneously taught that because God is spiritual and holy and because the human body is corrupt, the two could never meet. This brought them into very heretical ideas concerning the person of Christ and to grave moral errors concerning their own conduct. First, they could not conceive that Jesus Christ came in the flesh. Secondly, they felt that as long as the flesh was sinful, and God was interested therefore only in the spirit, moral laxity was permissible. All manner of sin was thus condoned. Now Gnosticism as a system has passed away. But the sin issue surely has not. To us, even as Christians, sin is an ever-present quandary. Moreover, if we do not learn how to deal with sin as it invades our experience, we will discover that vital fellowship with God is just as unreal a dream for us as it was for the Gnostics. We must never forget, as already emphasised, that God is light and cannot sanction sin.

Now how are we to deal with the problem of sin? This is the basic issue, for this and this alone is what disrupts communion with God. The fundamental truth to see is in verse 7: 'if we walk in the light, as he is in the light, we have fellowship with one another, and the blood of Jesus his Son cleanses us from all sin.' Obviously, the key phrase in the verse is the final statement where John says the blood of Jesus, God's Son, *continually* cleanses us Christians from all sin. (That is the force of the verbal tense John uses.) And this simply means, as is quite evident, that if we are to walk in the light we must constantly be cleansed by the power of Christ's forgiveness. Could it be that our proclamation of the death of Christ as the remedy for the sinful life has been restricted to just the historical past? Surely John is telling us here that Christians are to be constantly, daily cleansed by the blood of Christ. The death of Christ was not efficacious merely on the day of conversion. His sacrifice is to be effectual, as it were,

every day. Of course, as Alfred reminds us, it is sancti-
fication, not justification, that John is speaking of. But
Christians must learn the importance of this work of
God in their experience and recognise the centrality of
the daily cleansing from sin by Christ. Actually, it is not
going outside scriptural emphasis to say that walking
with God can only be realised in the context of constant, daily cleansing from our sins by the power and
forgiveness of Jesus Christ. This is what dispels our darkness so we can walk in the light.

Now I would imagine that much of what has been
said to this point will find a reasonably ready acceptance by most. Yet it is right here that nebulous thinking
begins to creep in. The bulk of us would probably agree
we need daily cleansing. It seems, however, that too
few have actually grasped the biblical concept of how
the believer is to deal with his sin in order that the blood
of Christ may be efficacious in cleansing him and thus
keep him in fellowship with God. This idea must be
investigated in a little more depth.

The first step in experiencing the cleansing of one's
sins centres in a proper understanding and evaluation
of how sin manifests itself in life's basic relationships.
It must be seen that sin usually presents itself in one of
three ways. First of all, there is sin that involves just
the individual Christian and his relationship to God.
Secondly, however, there may be sin that not only involves the Christian and God, it may also involve one's
relationship to another individual. Although every sin
is basically and essentially an affront to God, at times
other individuals are involved. Thirdly, there are inci-
dents when sin not only involves the Christian as an
individual in relationship with God, but is known and
open and thus involves a group of people such as the
Church.

Now for Christians to see their daily sins as a nebulous, indefinite whole tends to fail in moving one to deal
with them in God's prescribed manner. We must see

our sins specifically and individually, and to a greater or lesser degree we should categorise them as pointed out above. This is very important, for as sin is classified in one of these three categories, it can be dealt with accordingly—and scripturally, for the Bible deals with them on such a basis. Let us see how this works.

First, take the problem of sin as it involves just the believer and his personal relationship with God. What does the Bible say concerning this issue? The answer is found in 1 John 1:9, 'if we confess our sins, he is faithful and just, and will forgive our sins and cleanse us from all unrighteousness.' The word 'confess' is obviously the key term in this verse. In the language of the New Testament, it is a most interesting word. It is a compound word, comprised of the verb 'to say' and the adjective 'the same'. This clearly implies that to confess sins is 'to say the same as', or 'to assent to' the convicting Spirit of God that the particular thing in one's life of which the Spirit of God is convicting one actually is a sin. It must be recognised that the Spirit of God always deals with specifics in the Christian's life, not just with sin as a principle. That aspect of the problem for Christians was settled on the day of conversion. In other words, to confess sins scripturally is 'to concede to' or 'to agree with' the voice of God as He convicts us of some *particular* act of rebellion that it *truly is a sin*. Of course, this precludes that which we perhaps could call a 'blanket' confession of sins. For example, how often do we pray and hear other people pray, 'Lord, forgive me of all my sins!' Obviously, this is not the exact way the Scriptures state a Christian is to confess. To confess sins according to 1 John is to name them individually, one by one, agreeing with the Spirit of God that the particular act of which He convicts one is a sin. We do not commit our sins as a big nebulous whole; they are individual acts of rebellion. Thus the confession of our sins should not be in a general indefinable manner either. They should be confessed individually. This is why we must see them individually, as already stressed. Of course, this implies we must stay before God and walk in His presence and thus permit the Holy Spirit to search us out, convict us and place His finger on those particular deeds that constitute our sins. But having then acknowledged them before God in this prescribed manner, we have the assurance that the blood of Jesus cleanses them.

Perhaps it will be helpful to recount a personal experience here. Miss Bertha Smith, who has written a work entitled *Go Home and Tell* wherein she gives an account of the great Shantung revival in China in the 1930s, spoke in our church one time. Her message was along the line of confession and in the course of her address she urged us all to write what she called one's 'sin account'. She instructed us to take a piece of paper and on the left-hand column write down several numbers, then in the quiet of a secret place before God, to pray that the Holy Spirit would reveal every single thing in one's life that was displeasing to Him, that had grieved Him, and that had marred our fellowship with Him. Naturally, as a Christian, I wanted to be led into all that God had for me, so I took Miss Smith seriously. I did that which she had urged us to do; I made out my personal 'sin account'. Much to my humbling, the Spirit of God brought unconfessed things to my mind that I had committed months, even years ago. And the Holy Spirit so thoroughly searched me out that I found many unconfessed sins in my life. I wrote them down. Then, one by one, I brought them back before God and confessed them by acknowledging with the convicting Holy Spirit that those things were actually sins of which I was guilty. And when I confessed them like this, how precious the blood of Christ became.

Now this, of course, was not a time of morbid, neurotic introspection such as some seem to enjoy. It was not anything like that at all. This we must never permit ourselves to do. It was simply an honest evaluation of myself before God. Thus it brought a great release, not depression. Actually, it was one of the most liberating experiences of my Christian walk. A new fellowship with God was experienced.

But secondly, as we have seen, some of our sins may manifest themselves in relation to others as well as to God. In such an instance, merely to confess this sin to God alone is insufficient to experience the full release of Christ's forgiveness. To be sure we should confess them to God. But Jesus further stated in the Sermon on the Mount that if we have sinned against another and at the same time 'are offering your gift on the altar, and there remember that your brother has something against you, leave your gift before the altar and go; first be reconciled to your brother, and then come and offer your gift' (Matt. 5:23–4). Now I do not think we can avoid the simple truth presented here, that if we sin against another person and our fellowship is thus marred, restitution must be made to that person as well as to God. In the light of Jesus's statement, it is surely implied that to fail to acknowledge sins against individuals and to those individuals as much as it is possible under present circumstances and as God leads, then we cannot really expect deep fellowship with God or one another. I shall never forget the first time this truth came home to me. This was several years ago while I was pastor of a small church in Forth Worth, Texas. A young, deeply spiritual man preached on this theme in our church, and the Spirit of God bore witness to this truth to all of us. Many of us were compelled by the Spirit to put things right with different people.

Again, let it be clear that I am not speaking of a morbid introspective seeking and digging out of past sins in one's life. Still, I am thoroughly convinced that the Spirit of God can be grieved, and is grieved over unconfessed, unforsaken sin in our life. God is light, and we must take our darkness seriously. We must come to grips with ourselves as we truly are if we are to have the fullness of fellowship with God.

Moreover, as already implied, the seeking of forgiveness by those against whom we have sinned is certainly fundamental in our walking in fellowship with one another. Not only does it get our lives right with God, but also it keeps us right with one another. And after all, it is the only honest, ethical thing to do. If God expects us to confess our sins to Him to have fellowship with Him, certainly the principle applies to our human inter-personal relationships. If there could be something of a real openness among ourselves, if we could embrace one another in the arms of confession in the context of a true binding of our lives in love, understanding and forgiveness; our homes, our churches and our nation could be revolutionised. If fellowship with God and with one another means anything, it surely means this.

Finally, we found that sin at times manifests itself not simply against God alone, and perhaps not just against a single individual, but is open and others know of it. Or it may be we have some particular problem, secret or otherwise, where we have real difficulties. How is this issue to be dealt with? James tells us, 'Confess your sins to one another, and pray for one another, that ye may be healed' (Jas. 5 : 16). Does this mean that we are to confess openly our faults one to another? Does James mean to imply here that there are times when we should confess some of our sins to someone or perhaps even to a group in the church as well as to God? This seems to be his meaning. And surely there should be that person or group in the fellowship of believers to whom we can be quite open, honest and candid about ourselves. Is not this really what the true 'fellowship of kindred minds' means? Is not this the *koinonia* of love the New Testament talks about? The Church should be such a fellowship of love and understanding that we feel unthreatened to open our real selves to our brothers in Christ.

However, let us be most careful here. This is not to degenerate into an open airing of our 'dirty linen' to the whole world. Some have fallen into this trap. I should suppose that there are some areas of our lives that only God should ever know. At the same time, however, there is a need of genuine openness among God's people. We should drop the mask we tend to hide behind. And as a sensitivity to the Holy Spirit is developed and the fellowship of believers deepens He will surely open the door so that it will be clear what should be shared and with whom. One would hope all our churches could grow into such a fellowship of love, understanding and healing. Of course, if at times one's sins are so gross and well known that reproach is brought upon the entire church and the fellowship of the church broken thereby, then forgiveness should obviously be sought from the entire church. This is what lies behind the principle of church discipline that many congregations have apparently forgotten today. And this I should imagine, is what a public rededication of one's Christian life should really involve.

Now all of this that is said must be seen in the most positive light. For when it is sanely, maturely and scripturally approached, it is found to be a most liberating experience. When we become open with God and others, it strips off the mask and façade we tend to hide behind and thus we can become our real selves. Moreover, there has never been a deep spiritual awakening where this has not taken place. For as we confess our sins, that is confess them in this complete full sense that the Scriptures present, we can then claim the promise that God is faithful and just to forgive our sins and cleanse us from all unrighteousness. Being forgiven implies a debt remitted or sin dropped; the cleansing implies a stain bleached out. God not only forgives us but He cleanses us from the stain and thus liberates us to walk in the light as He is in the light. This is real fellowship with Christ and the essence of Christian community.

Victory over temptation
It is hoped that all that has been said to this point concerning sin and confession will not leave the impression that in Christ there is no victory over daily temptations and that our experience of God is nothing more than temptation, sin, confession, forgiveness, *ad infinitum*. The Scriptures are quite clear that God gives power over temptation as we walk in fellowship with Him. For example:

> Thanks be to God, who in Christ always leads us in triumph (2 Cor. 2 : 14).
> The law of the Spirit of life in Christ Jesus has set me free from the law of sin and death (Rom. 8 : 2).
> In all these things we are more than conquerors through him who loved us (Rom. 8 : 37).

The only conclusion that can be legitimately drawn from these verses is that in Christ there is victory over daily sin. But the issue is, how can that victory be achieved? We have surely learned that in our own strength we are powerless against some, if not many, temptations. What is the answer? It is important we find out! The holiness of our life is obviously quite dependent upon it.

The way of victory
John also deals with this issue in his first epistle, stating, 'This is the victory that overcomes the world, our faith' (1 John 5 : 4). Thus John tells us that the way of victory is the way of faith. It surely does not lie in our own self-effort or self-determination no matter how we may strive (Rom. 7 : 18). Victory comes only through faith. Paul presents the same idea when he states, 'above all taking the shield of faith, with which you can quench all the flaming darts of the evil one' (Eph. 6 : 16). Faith is the victory!

But faith must have an object. It will not do simply

to say, 'Have faith!' Genuine faith always has its foundation in truth. So it must be in the matter of victory over sin. In what reality then are we to place our faith? It is to be centred in the truth that the following passage presents:

> What shall we say then? Are we to continue in sin that grace may abound? By no means! How can we who died to sin still live in it? Do you not know that all of us who have been baptised into Christ Jesus were baptised into his death? We were buried therefore with him by baptism into death, so that as Christ was raised from the dead by the glory of the Father, we too might walk in newness of life.
> We know that, that our old self was crucified with him so that the sinful body might be destroyed, and we might no longer be enslaved in sin. For he who has died is freed from sin. But if we had died with Christ, we believe that we shall also live with him. For we know that Christ being raised from the dead will never die again; death no longer has dominion over him. The death he died he died to sin, once for all, but the life he lives he lives to God. So you also must consider yourselves dead to sin and alive to God in Christ Jesus.
> Let not sin therefore reign in your mortal bodies, to make you obey their passions. Do not yield your members to sin as instruments of wickedness, but yield yourselves to God as men who have been brought from death to life, and your members to God as instruments of righteousness. For sin will have no dominion over you, since you are not under law but under grace. (Rom. 6:1–14)

Now can we see the impact of what Paul is saying here? He is telling us that if a man is dead he is free from sin. But at the same time, if we are dead we will be of no value to Christ's service here on earth. If we could only be dead and alive at the same time that would solve our dilemma. But surely that is quite unthinkable, we retort! Yet it is right here that Paul makes a startling statement. He lays down the principle that because of our union with Christ, whereby we have been made one with Him, we have shared in our Lord's death on the cross. Therefore, we are to understand that we have actually died with Christ to sin. In a spiritual sense— yet in a very real way—when Christ died on the cross, we died with Him. When He gained the victory by His blood, we shared in that victory by death. The rationality behind this is that God sees us as already *in Him*. (The concept of 'in Christ' is the key to Pauline theology.) What He experienced, therefore, we have experienced. Thus we are already dead. And as a result we are free from sin's dominion over us. It is no longer our master; our 'old man' has been crucified with Christ (Gal. 2:20). Furthermore, not only have we died with Christ and shared in that experience of death, but because we are in Him we have also been spiritually resurrected with Him. We live because He lives. We are now animated by the resurrected life of our Lord in the person of His Holy Spirit. Can sin thus lord it over us? It absolutely cannot! We are dead to it and alive to God.

Now we must recognise that this truth does not appeal to one's human logic. It is most difficult to realise these truths as we look at our real selves. Yet God says it is true, and by faith we accept it. In actuality, it is only faith that can grasp this tremendous reality. *But therein lies victory.* As one author has pointedly expressed it:

> . . . when Christ died on the cross to sin, we were identified with Him in that death to sin. That is we died *with* Him. By our union with Him in His death, we were freed from the penalty of sin and emancipated from the power of sin. All our sanctification therefore must be traced to, and rests upon,

the atoning sacrifice of our Lord Jesus Christ. The cross of Christ is the efficient cause of deliverance from the power of sin. Freedom from the dominion of sin is a blessing we may claim by faith, just as we accept pardon.[2]

Here is how this principle works in one's everyday experience: Let us say we are met by one of our old weaknesses. We have striven to overcome it but with little success. Now, however, we realise our identification with Christ in His death and resurrection and by faith in that fact we say, 'This sin has no more power over me. I am dead to it.' Then in faith we look to God alone for the victory, and the resurrected life (the Holy Spirit) within us gives complete victory over the temptation. Faith in the fact of our death to sin and a vital look of faith to God is the answer. Thus we live in a new freedom never before experienced. Faith is the victory that overcomes the world. Not only in eternity are we delivered from the penalty and presence of sin, but now by faith we are saved from its power.

Now this is what it means to live a holy life; we walk in actual fellowship with the living Christ, daily being cleansed when we err but exercising constant faith in our identification with Him and looking to Him we achieve victory. He resides within us and we are in Him. Thus He simply lives His life out through us. And that quality of life cannot be anything but powerful in Christian mission, for it is not our life as such, rather it is Christ's life that is manifest. This is a marvellous truth! And it can be an experiential reality for all Christians. This now leads us to discuss the resource that is ours in

The power of the Holy Spirit
The work of the Holy Spirit must be seen for our immediate purposes in a two-fold sense. First, God imparts the person and power of the Holy Spirit to the believer

to make his life holy. One simply cannot live a holy life apart from the Holy Spirit. This we have already made clear. Secondly, it is the purpose of the Holy Spirit to demonstrate His power through the believer thus making Christian service effective and fruitful. As R. A. Torrey has correctly pointed out:

> The Holy Spirit is the person who imparts to the individual believer the power that belongs to God. This is the Holy Spirit's work in the believer, to take what belongs to God and make it ours. All the manifold power of God belongs to the children of God as their birthright in Christ. 'All things are yours' (1 Cor. 3:21). But all that belongs to us as our birthright in Christ becomes ours in actual and experimental possession through the Holy Spirit's work in us as individuals. To the extent that we understand and claim for ourselves the Holy Spirit's work, to that extent do we obtain for ourselves the fullness of power in Christian life and service that God has provided for us in Christ.[3]

In the light of these truths, it is obvious if one is to be effective in mission one must be properly related to the Holy Spirit.

What then is the scriptural principle of our relationship to the Spirit of God? In a word, how can we relate ourselves to Him so that He will give us power to live and serve Christ successfully? First let it be said that *all* believers are indwelt by the Holy Spirit and sealed by His stamp. This is clear from the New Testament. But the Scriptures also made it abundantly clear that Christians are also to be *filled* with the Holy Spirit. A believer is not to be merely a possessor of the Spirit, he is to be filled with the Spirit as well. And this is that relationship with God's Spirit that makes service powerful. This is forcefully brought out in the following passages of Scripture:

And behold, I send the promise of my Father upon you; but stay in the city, until you are clothed with power from on high (Luke 24:49).

But you shall receive power when the Holy Spirit has come upon you; and you shall be my witnesses in Jerusalem and in all Judea and Samaria and to the end of the earth (Acts 1:8).

And they were all filled with the Holy Spirit and began to speak in other tongues, as the Spirit gave them utterance (Acts 2:4).

And when they had prayed, the place in which they were gathered together was shaken; and they were all filled with the Holy Spirit and spoke the word of God with boldness (Acts 4:31).

And do not get drunk with wine, for that is debauchery; but be filled with the Spirit (Eph. 5:18).

It is obvious that God desires His people to be Spirit-filled Christians. Moreover, besides this tremendous weight of Scriptures—and there are many other passages as well—effective men of God give testimony to the validity of the concept of living a Spirit-filled life. For example, R. A. Torrey said, 'I was led to seek the baptism [filling] with the Holy Spirit, because I became convinced from the study of the Acts of the Apostles that no one had a right to preach the gospel until he had . . .' Charles G. Finney wrote, 'I was powerfully converted on the morning of the 10th of October, 1821. In the evening of the same day I received overwhelming baptisms [infillings] of the Holy Ghost.' A. T. Pierson said concerning his ministry after having been filled with the Spirit, 'I have seen more conversions and accomplished more in eighteen months since I received that blessing than in the eighteen years previous.'

But how does one receive the fullness of the Spirit and walk in His daily annointing? First one must confess and forsake all of his known sins. The heart, as much as we can know it, must be cleansed by the blood of

Christ (1 John 1:9). This principle we have already discussed. Then, one must surrender himself without reservation to Jesus Christ as Lord of life (Rom. 12:1–2). Finally, one should pray and simply trust God to do the work of filling (Luke 11:13). Actually, it is that simple. The very moment we confess all known sins (we all have unknown sins and can hardly confess these), surrender totally to Christ and trust God to fill us with His Spirit, He will surely meet our need and we will become a Spirit-filled Christian. Simple, yet how profound!

Now there is a definite relationship between being filled with the Spirit and daily walking with Christ as we discussed earlier. To grasp this we must first recognise that being filled with the Spirit is not a once-for-all experience as is the case concerning conversion. Further, it is not something that brings one into a state of perfection as some teach. Moreover, there is not one particular 'gift of the Spirit' one must receive to know he has been filled. God may give any gift He chooses as we have discussed in Chapter 3. It is not necessarily even an emotional experience. The point is, being filled with the Spirit is an experience that we need *each day we live*. As someone has said, we are 'leaky vessels' and we thus need to be refilled every day. This is why Paul said in Ephesians 5:8 (literally) '*continue* to be filled with the Spirit'. Being filled with the Spirit is a continuing experience. In other words, as we moment by moment walk with Christ, we daily come to Him as empty vessels to a full fountain to have our cup made full and running over with His Spirit. Now if we fail to walk with Christ, we will fail to come to Him for the divine infilling of His Holy Spirit, and we are thus impotent in His service and we lose the conscious glow of Christ's presence. To walk with God, therefore, is to walk in the continual infilling of His power. And obviously, when this is one's perpetual experience, he is bound to exemplify the power of a holy life and the dynamic of the Holy Spirit will work through him to make his service effective.

Furthermore, when we walk in the Holy Spirit's fullness many promises of the Scriptures can be claimed:

In the Holy Spirit we are set free from the law of sin and death (Rom. 8:2).

In the Holy Spirit we are strengthened in the inward man (Eph. 3:16).

In the Holy Spirit we find God's leading (Rom. 8:14).

In the Holy Spirit we bear fruit (Gal. 5:22-3).

In the Holy Spirit we are led into all truth (John 16:13).

In the Holy Spirit we learn to pray effectively (Eph. 6:18).

In the Holy Spirit we can communicate the truth to others (1 Cor. 2:15).

In the Holy Spirit we can evangelise in power (Acts 2:4-41).

Thus it can be correctly concluded that apart from a vital relationship to the Spirit of God, one can hope for little magnetism about his life or little power in his ministry. We simply cannot evangelise without the Spirit's work through us towards the unbelieving. A proper relationship with the Spirit of God is vital for mission.

Moreover, it is the Holy Spirit that inspires and develops in God's people

The power of a holy passion

It was David Brainerd, the great missionary to the American Indians, who said, 'I cared not where or how I lived or what hardships I went through so that I could but gain souls for Christ. While I was asleep I dreamed of these things, and when I awoke the first thing I thought of was this great work. All of my desire was for the conversion of the heathen and all my hope was in God.' In a similar spirit, Thomas Chalmers prayed, 'Recall the twenty-one years of my service; give me back its shipwreck, give me its standings in the face of death, give me it surrounded by fierce savages with spears and clubs, give it back to me with clubs knocking me down, give all this back to me, and I will be your missionary still.'

This is the attitude God honours. And this is the kind of passion that communicates to people. As John Wesley is reported as saying, 'Get on fire for God and people will come and watch you burn.' The passion for men that the Holy Spirit imparts is not to be quenched. Of course, I do not refer to a shallow vociferous approach to all we do, but to 'play it cool' in reaching men for Christ can be most damaging to evangelistic outreach. God desires His evangelists to be burdened, concerned, enthusiastic and zealous to spread the good news to the millions who truly desperately need to hear the message. And this attitude the Holy Spirit will instil as we seek His strength, wisdom and compassion. One would hope that all Christians could become so committed to the evangelistic task that such a passion would grip the entire Church. And if this situation is ever to develop, I suppose it must first begin with the pastor-evangelist.

The power of prayer

Prayer is another tremendous resource of power about which little perhaps need be said here. It is not that the theme is in any sense secondary. On the contrary, it is vital. The reason for saying little here is that so much fine material has already been produced on the subject that anything this author could contribute would be of little additional value. Let it simply be said, therefore, that prayer is essential to spiritual power in one's life and ministry. We get what we claim by faith in prayer. Every great spiritual movement has been conceived, born and matured in intercession. Whether it be Jacob, centuries ago, wrestling in prayer by the river Jabbok or the recent revival that has come to many American college and seminary campuses; through the millenniums of God's dealings with men, prayer has been the key that opens the treasure house of God's power. Probably one of our basic problems today is that 'you have not because you ask not' (Jas. 4:2). But all this we know. The issue is that we begin to pray and lead the entire Church to pray. Renewal and effective evangelism waits on the power of prayer. It is a vast resource for all Christians.

The power of the Word of God

The 'good seed' that falls in the ground and brings forth fruit is the Word of God. And it is a word of power: 'Is not my word like fire, says the Lord, and like a hammer which breaks the rock in pieces?' (Jer. 23:29). Space precludes an excursion into the interesting and relevant theological field of revelation and inspiration. What is important to realise at this point is simply that the Christian has tremendous resources in the power of our message. As Paul said, 'I am not ashamed of the gospel, it is the power of God for salvation to everyone who has faith' (Rom. 1:16).

Now the Bible itself has much to say about the power of the word in the hands of the Holy Spirit.

It is the instrument of the Spirit in conversion (Jas. 1:8).

It produces faith (Rom. 10:17).

It is the means of cleansing (Eph. 5:25–6).

It is that which builds one up in Christ (Acts 20:32).

It is a source of wisdom (Ps. 119:130).

It gives the assurance of eternal life (1 John 5:13).

These realities were brought home to me on an occasion when a pastor friend was speaking to a group of young people. He faithfully presented the gospel and at the conclusion of his message he quoted that word of Paul in 2 Corinthians 2:6: 'Behold, now is the day of salvation.' As the group was leaving a young man came to him and said, 'I had no intention of giving myself to Christ, but when you said now is the day of salvation, it really hit me. I want to become a Christian now.' It is quite true that 'the word of God is living and active, sharper than any two-edged sword' (Heb. 4 : 12).

So the Christian who desires to win others should realise he has a most powerful weapon in this warfare. Thus one can unashamedly and positively present the good news in the full assurance that God will honour His word of power and use it to speak to the hearts of the hearers. The proclaimer honours God when he honours God's word by forthrightly in faith declaring it. This is why we spent some time discussing the basic *kerygma*, for that is the good message God's Spirit uses to bring men to faith in Christ. One need not rely on human wisdom and ingenuity alone. As a matter of fact, if he does, he forsakes a great source of power that is at his disposal. It is the word of God alone that is the sword of the Spirit (Eph. 6 : 17).

In the final analysis, it is probably correct to sum it all up by emphasising the resource in

The power of a committed life

God's action through the life of the Christian waits for that life to be surrendered to His will and purpose. Knowledge comes through committal (John 7 : 17); prayer is dependent upon a surrendered will (1 John 3 : 23); one's joy and winsome testimony is based on a yieldedness to God's authority (John 15 : 10–11) and the Holy Spirit empowers only those who present themselves unreservedly to God's desire (Acts 5 : 32).

Even the psychologists tell us of the unifying influence and powerful impact of being committed to a great cause. And the world waits for those who are committed; committed to God and the evangelisation of the world. Moreover, the mission task that God lays upon His people is such that only the resource and power of a deep committal to the *missio Dei* will see it accomplished. May God bring us all into that relationship with Himself. The world waits!

1. Gavin Reid, *The Gagging of God*, p. 57.

2. Steven Barabas, *So Great Salvation* (New York, Fleming H. Revell), p. 88–9 (italics mine).

3. R. A. Torrey, *How to Obtain Fullness of Power* (London, Lakeland Paperbacks, 1955), p. 31.

Appendix: A Church Survey

Perhaps as never before, for the sake of its evangelistic task if not its own life, the Church needs to take a fresh look at itself. It is this 'fresh look' that motivates the suggestion that the local church conducts a 'diagnostic survey' of itself. The purpose of such a survey is to evaluate objectively the life of a local church in order that its ministry and witness may become more effective. All sincere Christians surely desire to see the life and ministry of their church enhanced, but before this happens it may be essential to 'overhaul' aspects of the present church programme. Such an undertaking calls for objectivity, honesty and not a little bravery. The outline that follows will provide in broad terms something of a guideline for the conducting of such a survey. It seems clear that if we can come to understand just where we are in local church life, we can see more clearly where we need to go. Spiritual insight and adaptability are of course required, but the following notes and questions should prove helpful in this important endeavour.

1 The setting of goals or aims

The first vital step, asking these questions:

What is the essential mission of the Church, and how does it relate to our local church?

How should this mission affect the aims and plans of our local church, and does it actually do so?

What should be, therefore, the aims of our local church?

Are the church members conscious of these aims?

Do these aims *govern* the development of the church programme, and the organisations and their functions? If not, why? Do we understand that the basic aim of the Church *must* be the foundation for building the local church programme?

II Surveying the community

The second step

Prepare a map of the community, indicating by a coloured line the area surrounding the church. (Show church location.)

Prepare a brief description of the church territory, e.g. location, type of housing, age, industrial or residential, racial patterns, sub-cultural groups, institutions, problems related to its environment, etc. This will take some study.

Describe the community needs that should be met by the church.

Evaluate the effectiveness of the church in meeting the needs of its immediate community. What can and should be done to meet these needs?

III Surveying the organisational life of the church

The third step

GENERAL

Summarise briefly the history of the church and how this relates (if it does) to the present church life.

Evaluate and criticise the church's constitution and/or by-laws if it has any.

Study the church property and buildings. What long (or short) term plans should be made by the church concerning its location and future building needs? How adequate are the present buildings to meet the needs of the community? What repairs or changes are vital for the present *and* future? Are we using the present buildings to the best advantage in accordance with the church's message and ministry? What other building resources are available?

WORSHIP

What is the programme of church music? Is this vital aspect of church life given proper interest and work?

Study the church services of worship. Are they relevant? Is the language used that which communicates? Are the church ordinances meaningfully observed? What is being done to educate in worship? Are the services 'alive'? What can be done? What should be kept? Do we understand what is the relationship between worship and mission?

EVANGELISM

Describe the outreach of the church. What is actually being done now? Is there an evangelistic committee? What is the record of successful outreach over the past ten years? Are the church organisations involved in evangelism? How conscious are the church members of the need and centrality of evangelism? Are the worship services effectively evangelistic, etc.?

PASTORAL CARE

How are members received into the church? What does the church do to integrate new church members into the total church programme? What plans are there for conserving and training new members in the Christian life and church life? How adequate and useful are the membership rolls? What action is taken over inactive members?

Evaluate church ministries. What services are rendered to family life—before and after marriage? What about the church's 'crisis' ministry, i.e. in times of death, serious illness, birth, etc.? What about the problems of broken families, delinquency, crimes, when these occur in the life of the church members or in the community, etc.? To what extent is the whole church involved in pastoral care?

CHRISTIAN EDUCATION

Evaluate the overall effectiveness of the church's educational programme. This should include the work of the Sunday School, women's work, men's organisations, etc. The question must be asked: Is our church truly educating people in the Bible? Is there any segment of our people not receiving teaching in the Scriptures? If so, what can be done? Have we considered an 'all-age' Bible training programme? *Are organisations in line with the mission?* Is there a leadership training programme? Is the laity being taught and equipped for ministry?

STEWARDSHIP

Study the church plan for promoting and practising Christian stewardship. Describe and evaluate the plan of church finance. What emphasis is placed on this important aspect of dedication? What portion of the membership gives regularly? What is done to increase this number? How badly hindered is the life and ministry of the church because of poor stewardship? Why is there a reluctance to emphasise stewardship? Is this 'play-down' right? How about a stewardship campaign? Does the church spend its monies in such a way as to encourage giving? Should we consider a unified budget scheme?

RECREATIONAL AND SOCIAL MINISTRIES

Evaluate church recreation, for old and young, and other specialised activities, e.g. drama, youth clubs, holiday clubs, etc. What sort of impact are we making on the community?

LEADERSHIP

Evaluate leadership participation. What proportion of church members have some definite place of service in the church programme? In the light of the study of the church organisations, how adequate is the church leadership? How are leaders discovered? What training, if any, do they receive to do their job effectively?

ADMINISTRATIVE

Study the problem of co-ordination and correlation. Is the church well integrated? How do the organisations relate to one another and help one another? Is the leadership of the church's total programme unified and harmonious? Are there 'churches within the church'? Are there too many overlappings and duplications of activities and functions? *Do all of the organisations live, minister, develop, function, and serve in the light of the mission of the Church?* Is there any overall group co-ordinating the whole church life? Is too much power vested in a few? Study the administrative facilities of the church. Is there adequate equipment, e.g. duplicator, typewriter, etc.? Does the pastor do an unfair amount of this work? Could the load be shared by others? Are good records kept? Are they used and found helpful to a better church life?

PUBLIC RELATIONS

Study and evaluate the promotional and publicity plans of the church. Are the monies used wisely and effectively? Do these plans 'grab' people in their interest, i.e. do they truly communicate?

IV Surveying the church leadership

The fourth step

Note: It is understood that in undertaking this task the spirit of understanding and of Christ must be manifest.

Moreover, leaders of the church will have shared considerably in gathering the other information in the survey.

Interviewing the pastor. How does the minister see his role? How did he face the problem of getting started in the church? How does he cope with the problems of relationships? How does he feel about the need of church administration? How does he feel about the evangelistic enterprise? What does the pastor consider his primary function in the life of the church? Is he able to fulfil that role? If not, why not? What plan does he have to find time for leisure and for his family? What would he like to see changed in the church?

Interviewing the official body (deacons, stewards, elders, etc.). How do they see their role? What do they consider to be their relationship to the pastor and church? What are their particular problems? What do they feel hinders the life and effectiveness of the church? Are their attitudes in line with the New Testament?

Interviewing the church lay-leaders. What do they feel is their role in the life of the church? Do they feel they were properly enlisted? Do they feel they are receiving proper training for their tasks? How do they feel about the specific organisation in which they serve? Do they feel overworked with too many responsibilities, etc.?

It is well to interview at random a few representative lay-members (such as a young person, an old person, even children) to get something of the reaction of the average person who just comes but takes no active part in leadership. Do they feel everything is done by the few? Is it so? Do they feel mere spectators? What would they like changed?

SUMMARY AND SUGGESTIONS

It is obvious that the purpose of such an extensive survey is the assessment of a local church's life. All of the organisations will have to be looked into in depth and evaluated. Perhaps an analogy could be found in an extensive physical examination that a doctor would carry out on a patient for the purpose of diagnosing ills so that the proper remedy may be found. This undertaking must be the work of several. Perhaps a group of the key leadership in the church would be the logical group to do the work. As already emphasised, it must be done with objectivity, honesty, bravery, and above all, in the spirit of helpfulness, understanding and love. Much discussion and much prayer must go into the venture. *The whole idea is for a local church to understand itself in the light of the great mission of the Church and to attempt to bring itself and all of its activities in line with that mission.* Moreover, it is hoped that such a survey will not just be put on paper and laid to rest. It should form a working plan to change and update the whole life of the church. And in the end it would be hoped that God's Spirit will so lead in the matter that His blessings will result in a far more effective ministry for the church and many more won to dedication to Christ and His Kingdom. Granted, the church survey is the negative diagnostic side. Now the Church must build a great new programme to the glory of God. That is the positive side each local church must undertake. But the rewards are well worth the extensive effort.

Bibliography

Listed below are several works on the theme of mission that are not mentioned in the chapter notes.

Wm Barclay, *Fishers of Men* (London, Epworth Press, 1966).

Arthur H. Bird, *Adventures in Evangelism* (Worthing, Henry E. Walter Ltd, 1968).

James Burns, *Revivals, Their Laws and Leaders* (Grand Rapids, Baker Book House, 1960).

A. W. Chirgwin, *The Bible in World Evangelism* (New York, Friendship Press, 1954).

Gaines S. Dobbins, *Evangelism According to Christ* (Nashville, Broadman Press, 1949).

Charles G. Finney, *Memoirs* (New York, Flemming H. Revell Co., 1876).

C. Wade Freeman, *The Doctrine of Evangelism* (Nashville, Benson Printing Co., 1957).

James Leo Garrett, Jr, *Evangelism for Discipleship* (Louisville, Southern Baptist Theological Seminary, 1964).

Bryan Gilbert, *Continuous Evangelism* (London, Oliphants, 1969).

Eugene Myers Harrison, *How to Win Souls* (Wheaton, Scripture Press Foundation).

The Islington Conference, *Mission in the Modern World* (London, Patmos Press, 1968).

E. Stanley Jones, *Conversion* (London, Hodder and Stoughton, 1959).

T. A. Kantonen, *The Theology of Evangelism* (Philadelphia, Muhlenberg Press, 1954).

Roland Q. Leavell, *Evangelism Christ's Imperative Commission* (Nashville, Broadman Press, 1954).

Paul E. Little, *How to Give Away Your Faith* (London, Inter-Varsity Press, revised edn. 1971).

W. L. Muncy, Jr, *New Testament Evangelism for Today* (Kansas City, Central Seminary Press, 1946).

Wm G. McLoughlin, Jr, *Modern Revivalism* (New York, The Ronald Press, 1959).

J. I. Packer, *Evangelism and the Sovereignty of God* (London, Inter-Varsity Press, 1961).

H. Cecil Pawson, *Personal Evangelism* (London, Epworth Press, 1968).

W. Dayton Roberts, *Revolution in Evangelism* (London, Scripture Union, 1967).

Paulus Scarpff, *History of Evangelism* (Grand Rapids, Wm B. Eerdmans Publishing Co., 1966).

Ron Smith, *The A.B.C. of Personal Evangelism* (Bromley, The Fishers Fellowship).

Samuel Southard, *Pastoral Evangelism* (Nashville, Broadman Press, 1962).

Wm B. Sprague, *Lectures on Revivals of Religion* (London, The Banner of Truth Trust, 1958).

Wm Warren Sweet, *Revivalism in America* (Nashville, Abingdon Press, 1944).

John Tanburn, *Open House* (London, Falcon Books, 1970).

Mendell Taylor, *Exploring Evangelism* (Kansas City, Beacon Hill Press, 1964).

Charles B. Templeton, *Evangelism for Tomorrow* (New York, Harper and Brothers, 1957).

George W. Weber, *The Congregation in Mission* (Nashville, Abingdon Press, 1964).

Bernard A. Weisberger, *They Gathered at the River* (Chicago, Quadrangle Paperbacks, 1966).